Washington County PARANORMAL

A WISCONSIN LEGEND TRIP

J. Nathan Couch

J. NATHAN COUCH

Copyright © 2019 J. Nathan Couch

All rights reserved. No part of this publication may be reproduced or transmitted in any form or by any means, electrical or mechanical, including photocopy, recording, or any information storage or retrieval system, without the permission from the publisher.

Library of Congress Control Number: 2012914422
ISBN: 1478379553
ISBN-13: 978-1478379553

Printed in the United States by Createspace

First Published by J. Nathan Couch in 2012
West Bend, Wisconsin
wcwiparanormalproject@yahoo.com
www.jnathancouch.com

Interior Layout: J. Nathan and Jessica Sawinski Couch

Exterior Cover Design: Charlie Hintz of Mental Shed Studios

Dedication

This book is dedicated to:

My wife, Jessica, for helping me achieve my potential;

My parents, William T. and Lois Couch—I wish you could have read this, Mom;

Amanda, Dusty, and Van for following me to each and every haunt…and running away with me from each and every one as well.

Contents

Forward by John Edward Radcliffe	i
Acknowledgments	iii
Introduction	iv
Map	ix

Section 1: Northern Washington County

Boltonville: Jay Road	Pg 2
Farmington: Lizard Mound County Park	Pg 7
Kewaskum: Goat Man Road	Pg 14
West Bend: AmericInn	Pg 17
West Bend: Eisenbahn Trail	Pg 19
West Bend: Healing Elements Day Spa	Pg 24
West Bend: Kettle Moraine YMCA Farm House	Pg 27
West Bend: Newark Cemetery	Pg 30
West Bend: Old Courthouse Museum	Pg 33
West Bend: Old Sheriff's Residence and Jail	Pg 38
West Bend: Old St. Joseph's Community Hospital	Pg 43
West Bend: Old City Hall	Pg 45
West Bend: Poplar Inn	Pg 48

West Bend: Rainbow Lake	Pg 50
West Bend: Regner Park	Pg 53
West Bend: Restat Building	Pg 57
West Bend: Silver Creek Apartments	Pg 60
West Bend: University of Wisconsin-Washington County and Ridge Run County Park	Pg 62
West Bend: Wallace Lake	Pg 67
West Bend: Washington County Memorial Park	Pg 69
West Bend: Washington House	Pg 72
West Bend: West Bend Theatre	Pg 77

Section II: Central Washington County

Hartford: Kettle Moraine Road	Pg 82
Hartford: Schauer Arts and Activities Center	Pg 84
Jackson: County Road P	Pg 89
Jackson: Hasmer Lake	Pg 91
Jackson: Jackson Marsh	Pg 93
Polk: Cedar Creek Cemetery	Pg 95
Slinger: Elementary School and High School	Pg 98

Section III: Southern Washington County

Erin: Holy Hill	Pg 102
Erin: State Highway 167	Pg 105
Erin: Tally Ho Pub and Grill	Pg 108

Germantown: Berg's Saloon	Pg 113
Germantown: Dheinsville Settlement Park Intersection	Pg 115
Germantown: Madam Belle's Silver Dollar Saloon	Pg 117
Germantown: Mary Buth Farm	Pg 121
Hubertus: Fox and Hounds Restaurant	Pg 124
Hubertus: Hogsback Road	Pg 127
Selected Bibliography	Pg 131
About the Author	

Foreword

I need to warn you. Before you read this book, you might want to learn my Scottish mother's favorite prayer:

> From ghoulies and ghosties
> And long-leggedy beasties
> And things that go bump in the night,
> Good Lord, deliver us.

Who doesn't like a good ghost story? You can take a more modern approach and call it "paranormal activity," if you choose. It should be noted I still keep a nightlight in my bedroom and prefer to turn the lights on before I enter the barn.

When you first explore *Washington County Paranormal*, you will be amazed at the prolific catalogue of occurrences Nathan has documented at three dozen different sites. Keep telling yourself this is Washington County in Wisconsin, not the Borgo Pass in Transylvania.

My Celtic family would call these places where this world meets the spirit world "thin spots."

Nathan also presents sightings of bizarre creatures of legend, such as the Goat Man and the Bearwolf, along with the locations in which they've been encountered.

Those of you who live near these locations will probably find yourselves seeing them through new eyes. For the rest of you, Nathan provides driving directions so you can locate each of these sites and experience them for the first time for yourself. I'd suggest you forgo nocturnal visits to the more remote spots. Of course, I don't believe in ghosts or "paranormal activity" myself, or do I?

Nearly thirty years ago, we purchased Eiscirhame, a small farmstead located three-quarters of a mile down a dirt road from Route Y in Trenton. It was in ruins and had a spotted history. During the Civil War, it had been a tobacco farm, and the drying shed still stands attached to the dairy barn. It was converted around 1890 to dairy, and the huge barn was raised from local timber. After the Second World War, it became a rental property and spent its last years as a horse farm. It was abandoned around 1977 and left to decay. The renovation started in the early spring and took about five months. During that time, we began moving our household from New York State. We decided to use the barn for storage since the house was being rebuilt. One day, we pushed the heavy farm machinery stored there aside to make room. Overnight, it moved back. We bought padlocks to secure the building and moved the machinery again. Again, it moved back. We switched the arrangement of specific items, and they moved back. So we stored the household goods in the basement of the farmhouse instead.

Now don't tell me I'm alone in this. You know there are ghosts even if you haven't met any.

—John Edward Radcliffe, Guild Storyteller and Author of *Storms of the Scottish Isles, Dark Tales of Creatures and Beings on the Remote Islands of the North Atlantic.*

Acknowledgments

The following is a poorly organized and very likely incomplete list of people who've helped me with this project in some manner or another. If your name's not listed, I'm a bonehead, and I sincerely apologize. Patricia Lutz, Jessica Sawinski Couch, and Heather Przybylski of the Washington County Historical Society; Robert Bernhagen and family; Shirley Walters; Marjorie Seyfert; Jane Goffin; April Shaw; Charlie Hintz of Mental Shed Studios; WisconsinSickness.com; Tim Freiss; Reuben Schmahl; Magaret Schmahl; Nancy Schilling-Genz; Eugene Wendleborn; Diane Lorenz; Sarah Philips; Catherine Sawinski; all Washington County Writers' Club members past and present; Dave Rank and the Moraine Writers' Guild; John Edward Radcliffe; Linda S. Godfrey; Mike Hoke, Kellie Wirtz, Scott Bares, Walter Skilling, and everyone else in the Paranormal Investigation and Research Society past or present; Alan Gee, Dan Cartwright, and the rest of the Wisconsin Area Paranormal Society; Alison Jornlin; Mike Huberty; Debra Hendrix; Randy Schultz and Robyn K. Wilkinson of the Schauer Arts and Activities Center; Chaz Hastings of the Tally Ho Pub and Grill; Jason Pipkorn of Madam Belle's Silver Dollar Saloon; the Germantown Historical Society; Nicolette Moldenhauer Kearns of Healing Elements Day Spa; The West Bend Community Memorial Library; The Poplar Inn; Dan Schneiter of the Fox and Hounds Restaurant; J. R. Turner; The Wisconsin Writers Association; An Idle Hour or Two; the patrons of the Downtown West Bend Ghost Walk; and you, for reading this book. If it weren't for you, this whole thing would have been pointless.

Introduction

I grew up in Cleveland, a small town in the foothills of Northeast Georgia's Blue Ridge Mountains. There was no movie theater or shopping mall, and you couldn't buy alcohol without driving a half an hour. In other words, there wasn't much to do. It's no wonder dinner-table discussions between the adults in my family often drifted into the realm of the bizarre. Photographs of my grandfather's ghost, sightings of lizard men, and rumors of Native American curses were subjects discussed as matter-of-factly as the weather. These topics scared me, perhaps even scarred me, but I couldn't stop listening. I needed to know every detail, no matter how many bad dreams it caused me. Thus began my obsession with the paranormal.

Life changes slowly in the mountains—if it changes at all. By the time I was a teen, the town still lacked the entertainment and stimulation for which I so desperately hungered. My friends and I had to find our thrills in unconventional ways. We spent countless nights getting lost on dusty, isolated back roads seeking adventure. If another kid told us a little girl's ghost played by the railroad tracks, we'd take our flashlights and go looking. Every time some old man said he'd seen a bigfoot shamble across the highway near his farm, we were quick to investigate.

Back then, there was no name for this type of fun. It was just something bored kids did to pass the time. These days, the activity is known as "legend-tripping," and with the popularity of paranormal tourism, it isn't just for boys lacking girlfriends anymore. Men, women, and children from all backgrounds now go in search of the paranormal.

I'm proud to say I haven't outgrown the preferred pastime of my youth. I still go hunting for the unexplained even though there are many years and many hundreds of miles separating me from that little town where I grew up. If anything, my status as a Wisconsin resident has nurtured my unique interests. The Badger State is rich in weirdness and rather openly acknowledges it. For the last several years, I've lived in West Bend, the county seat of Washington County. I've traveled all over this wonderful state visiting haunted bridges, abandoned cemeteries, and the various UFO capitals of Wisconsin—Elmwood, Belleview, and Dundee each claim the title. All the while, I wondered where the haunts and the monsters of Washington County were. Why was my new home

Introduction

devoid of such bizarre legends, which were in ample supply elsewhere in the Cheese State? When I first considered writing this book, I feared that there simply wouldn't be enough material. I had become aware of only a handful of sites in the county via books from my own personal library. The former Restat Building in West Bend, the bigfoot/bearwolf sightings near Holy Hill, and the Mary Buth Farm are all rather well known. However, two haunts and one cryptid would hardly fill an entire book. So I risked wasting my time and started a campaign on various social networking websites in search of legend trip–worthy locations. I was quickly inundated with haunted pubs, bottomless lakes, and demonic possessions. The book would be possible after all. It turns out there were plenty of Washington County legends. All I had to do was ask.

Regarding Sources

As stated above, I obtained much of the information about local legends and haunts from Washington County's residents. Each and every person who contacted me for this project shared genuine experiences that are utterly astonishing. When presenting these experiences, I have made every attempt to have an open mind and not cast judgment, no matter how mundane or sensational the story. I met the majority of these people in person and have no reason to doubt either their sanity or their integrity. In fact, I admire their bravery for sharing such experiences with an utter stranger. While most people who read a book of this nature will likely share my attitude, a few inevitably won't. Several of the people who spoke with me for the book wished to be identified by only their first name, an assumed name, or not at all. While using a witness's real and full name adds credibility, I completely understand their concerns and respect their privacy.

As far as historical information, I spent many hours at libraries and historical societies and have made every effort to document my sources and present accurate information. While I sincerely hope no one tries to use this book in any form of academic research, I certainly want readers to know where I obtained dates and histories.

Investigations

As part of the research process, I joined—and am still part of—a paranormal investigation team based out of Washington and Fond du Lac Counties called the Paranormal Investigation and Research Society

(PIRS). I made every attempt to investigate or visit the locations I've written about, but in some cases, it simply wasn't possible. We investigated several businesses, including the Tally Ho Pub and Grill in Erin and the Schauer Arts and Activities Center in Hartford. Some locations, such as Jay Road in Boltonville, were best investigated simply by driving down them. Many sites, including the Mary Buth Farm in Germantown, were inaccessible and were examined only in the historical and folkloric sense. Some people simply don't want a bunch of "ghost hunters" spending the night at their home or business.

Writing Style and Organization

This isn't the first legend-trip/paranormal guidebook written. In fact, there are many out there, and most of them are wonderful. My chief complaint with some of them (as a user, not as a fellow writer) is they're either extremely functional but tedious to read or entertaining but less than stellar in getting you to your destination. I've attempted to make this book both a collection of entertaining essays and an easy-to-use resource on the road. It's up to you, the reader, to decide if I've succeeded.

I've split the book into three sections: Northern, Central, and Southern Washington County. Within each section, I've organized the towns, cities, or villages alphabetically. The locations within a given city or town are then also organized alphabetically. Directions to each location follow each essay.

Driving Directions

Writing directions to these locations is difficult when you've no knowledge of whether your reader lives in Milwaukee or Minneapolis. I've tried to give directions to each location from somewhere that's easy to get to. You won't find driving directions to Erin from Chicago, but if you make it to Erin, this book should be able to get you to Holy Hill. Keep in mind, this world changes quickly. Roads are redesigned or renamed, and buildings get torn down. The directions found in this book were correct when I wrote them, but a year from now, who knows? Always bring a map, a GPS, or at the very least, a friend who knows which side of the tree moss grows on. I should also mention my wife, Jessica, was a great help in writing these directions. Being a writer, I don't get out as much as she does. Jessica's also very good with maps. Just ask her, and she'll tell you.

Introduction

Rules for the Rookie Legend Tripper

If you're a seasoned legend tripper, you likely already know the rules of conduct we all live by. However, it never hurts to brush up. One bad egg can ruin it for everyone. Here are the generally accepted guidelines for a responsible legend tripper:

- Never go on private property without permission. If it turns out the location you've arrived at is marked "No Trespassing," please *don't* break the law.
- Always be respectful of the locals. You're representing all your fellow legend trippers.
- Always take a buddy. Don't go wandering around looking for ghosts and monsters alone. If you actually encounter the Goat Man, you'll be glad your friend Steve was there. Also keep in mind there are plenty of "mundane" dangers to confront solo legend trippers, such as serial killers and other motorists. There is always safety in numbers.
- Never litter, steal, or vandalize. That should go without saying.
- Always take a flashlight, a cell phone, a map or GPS, a blanket, a first-aid kit, and some food and water. Always be prepared. Cars can break down, and people can be hurt or get lost.
- Never go into cemeteries at night unless you know you're allowed to. The majority close at sunset. Again, please don't break the law.
- Always tell someone if you actually get face-to-snout with the legend you're pursuing—especially writers like me.
- Never be disappointed if you don't encounter the legend. It's cliché, but I believe it to be true: it's not about the destination; it's about the journey.

Are These Locations Really Haunted?

Yes, according to various witnesses, websites, and oral tradition. However, the author of this book (me) makes no such claim. Even when I've investigated a location with PIRS, I've made no formal verdict. Why? Because science has yet to prove the existence of ghosts, goat men, or bearwolves. This book is for entertainment purposes only.

Will There Be Other Books?

I certainly hope so. Writing and researching this book has been an amazing experience. If you know of a legend trip in your hometown, don't hesitate to contact me at washingtoncountyparanormal.com!

Map

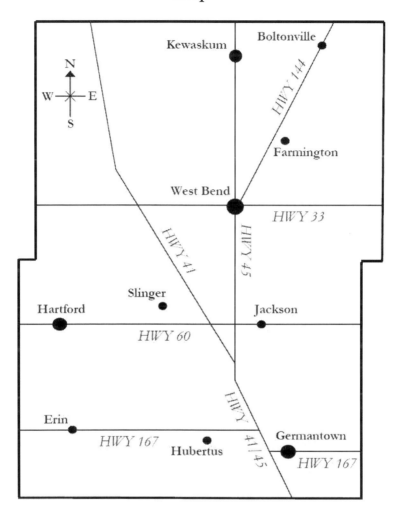

Washington County, Wisconsin

Section I: Northern Washington County

Boltonville: Jay Road

Jay Road—or "Seven Bridges Road" as it's unofficially known—is a twenty-five-mile length of road, which begins in Boltonville and continues east through Ozaukee County until it dead-ends at the shore of Lake Michigan. It's also home to two ghastly legends.

The Cat Lady

The "Old Cat Lady" has become a modern American archetype—a lonely, elderly woman in decline with nothing except a hoard of felines to keep her company. It's a stereotype that's become particularly negative in recent years with numerous stories in the news regarding pet hoarders and instances of animal abuse. Considering this, a more relevant legend than the Cat Lady of Jay Road will be hard to find.

A pack of vicious teens from the small unincorporated community of Boltonville grew weary of their quiet rural environment and began creating their own brand of cruel entertainment—tormenting the beloved cats of an old woman who lived alone on Jay Road. Horrified at their torture of her furry companions, she called the police, and a feud ignited.

The old woman and her pets became the targets of sadistic harassment, culminating in fatal arson. One fateful night, the teens set fire to the woman's house while she and most of her cats were still inside. When she awoke, the cats were yowling for their very lives. With no regard for her own well-being, she attempted to save them, but they were too frightened and too many in number. Refusing to abandon them, she stayed inside the house. As she burned alive, the old woman put a curse on the land where her house once stood. Her fearsome, charred form now roams Jay Road looking to haunt kids who're up to no good.

No version of the story I'd heard said where on Jay Road this tragedy took place. The legend does say that on certain nights, you can see her phantom house ablaze while her doomed cats flee into the night, aflame. One article about the legend in the *West Bend Daily News* featured interviews with many longtime Boltonville residents who'd never heard of a house fire down Jay Road. I assumed the entire story was mere fantasy, until I was contacted by a woman I'll call "L." about a house she once lived in on Jay Road.

> We lived there for two and a half years, but we didn't hear any stories about the Cat Lady until we had moved out. We knew a house had burned down to the foundation nearby. Its remains were still there. The landlord had told our kids to be careful around it. After it had burned, the landlord bought another house and moved it onto the property. That's where we lived.
>
> I would see cats from the corner of my eye on a chair. I would turn to look, and they were gone. [My daughter] would actually see one approach her and presume it was our house cat. One cat came to sit with her on the couch. When she noticed she could see right through it, it disappeared.
>
> [My oldest son] would see a little blond girl in his bedroom. One day, while home alone, he ran downstairs thinking he'd heard us return. He heard kids' voices, people coming up the deck stairs. But when he got to the kitchen, the whole house was quiet. No one else was home.
>
> The kitchen faucet would turn on by itself. We'd argue over who was going to turn it off.
>
> [My youngest son] would talk to someone on the stairs. I overheard him one day saying he wasn't allowed to run down the steps. "Besides even if I win, *you* always disappear!" he shouted. He used to come up to me at night to tell me he'd seen a little girl standing in the doorway of his room. She had sparkles and pretty lights around her, and she'd always leave out the window.
>
> My husband says we have a ghost cat [at our current house]. He feels it jumping on our bed at night and walking around. Maybe these things can follow you?

While L.'s former haunted house lacks many elements of the Cat Lady legend, it does support the story that a house on the road burned down and that phantom felines have been seen. Perhaps this is where the legend of the Cat Lady originated? If you're traveling down Jay Road at night and a cat crosses your path, look closely. You might be able to see right through it.

The Jogger

Just outside of Boltonville, the landscape along Jay Road turns to swamp. Cattails, old overturned canoes, and silt-clouded water edge right up alongside the road while thick woods stand just out of reach. One would be hard-pressed to find a more haunted-looking place. Even during summer at midday, this area seems a likely haunt for earthbound spirits. This is home to the second legend of Seven Bridges: the jogger.

Early one morning just before dawn, a young woman was jogging through the swamp. Along this expanse of road, there is no shoulder, only stagnant water. Headlights suddenly illuminated the night behind her. As the sound of the approaching vehicle grew nearer, she turned and looked over her shoulder. The car was weaving violently; the driver was clearly inebriated. The car swerved, and the girl was hit and launched into the water. The swamp claimed her, body and soul.

Sometimes visible as a wisp of fog, the young woman floats down the lonely road. Some will see the fog slowly take shape as they get nearer. Now, once again a beautiful young woman out for a nocturnal jog, she feels your headlights shining down on her. She turns and stops, frozen in terror. Your car strikes her, and she dissipates into the cool night air. Some versions of her legend go so far as to say that she appears in your backseat, and your car battery dies as she siphons its energy to materialize. In some versions of this legend, she's accompanied by the ghost of a white dog.

You'd think a road with such a tragic and terrifying reputation would be avoided at all costs, but traveling down Jay Road at night has become a rite of passage for area teens.

While hardly a teen, I myself have tempted fate and gone looking for the sad apparition of the Jay Road Jogger on numerous occasions. The most memorable expedition was one Sunday night in September 2009. My wife, Jessica, and I were restless. It was too early to go to sleep and too late to do anything else. We decided to go for a drive.

Section I: Northern Washington County

The weather was gloomy. The sun was setting, and the sky was shrouded. We began the trip rather aimlessly. I drove down whichever road seemed compelling at the time. Before long, we were on County Highway M, approaching Boltonville.

"You wanna go looking for ghosts?" my wife asked.

I replied with an enthusiastic "Yes!" This is just one of the many reasons why I married her.

As soon as we began to approach the swamp, the landscape grew misty and mysterious—not unusual for a swamp, but I couldn't help but imagine the curling clouds of mist taking on human shape as we slowly drove through.

Up ahead, a light appeared, but it wasn't a car's headlights. It was a singular light source. As we got closer, my pulse began to race. The light grew nearer and began to take shape—a human shape. The apparition was jogging down the westbound lane directly at us. We both screamed. I slammed on the brakes, my knuckles turning white as I gripped the steering wheel. It would have been the experience of a lifetime, except the apparition was no apparition, just an old man in a reflective jogging suit.

The conspiracy theorist in me likes to think he did this hoping to scare the pants off a couple of kids—or in this case, a bored young married couple—who were out looking for a thrill. However, it's much more likely he'd recently been diagnosed with high cholesterol.

First, we swore. Then we laughed. We drove home relieved and disappointed all at the same time. The Jay Road Jogger remains elusive, but as long as there are nights with nothing much to do, we'll keep looking.

Directions

From Milwaukee: Take HWY 41/45 to West Bend. Exit at HWY 33, and head east.

From Fond du Lac: Take HWY 41 south to Allenton. Exit at HWY 33, and head east.

From Madison: Take HWY 151 to Beaver Dam. Exit at HWY 33, and head east.

Once in West Bend: From HWY 33, turn north onto HWY 144 N/N Main Street. Follow HWY 144 to Boltonville. Turn right onto Jay Road.

Section I: Northern Washington County

Farmington: Lizard Mound County Park

Native American burial grounds and hauntings have strolled hand in hand through the dark wooded paths of American pop culture for a long time indeed. Find a location that holds, or once held, a Native American burial, and you'll soon find whispered allegations of paranormal activity. With that said, it should come as no surprise that the mysterious Lizard Mound County Park is supposed to be haunted.

The park is a cluster of mounds, many of them burial mounds, located in Hagner's Woods. They range in shape from simple linear and conical mounds to effigies of birds, panthers—now thought to be depictions of water spirits—and one particularly unique "lizard," though experts now largely agree it's actually a turtle.

The people who built these mounds are as mysterious as the mounds themselves. Commonly referred to as the "Effigy Mound Builders," they lived in Wisconsin and neighboring states between 700 CE and 1200 CE.

Today, the debate over the identity of these mound builders focuses on determining which of the modern-day Native American tribes' ancestors constructed these beautiful earthen works. However, there was a time when some doubted that the mounds were built by Native Americans at all. Since the natives who lived in the area of the mounds were no longer building them when Europeans first arrived in Wisconsin, it was assumed that some lost culture, or "race," had to have been responsible. Naturally, this "lost race" must have been eradicated by the current native population. I can't help but notice this theory of an established culture being displaced by a newer, more aggressive culture mirrored exactly what was happening as Europeans conquered North America.

Posited identities of the "lost race" ranged from the slightly plausible Aztecs to the nearly impossible lost tribe of Israel or the Atlanteans. Early twentieth-century West Bend writer and Washington County historian Carl Quickert subscribed to the "lost race" theory.

In the first volume of *Washington County, Wisconsin Past and Present* (1912), Quickert writes about the extraordinary discovery of enormous human bones near what is now Lizard Mound County Park. While collecting gravel for road construction, farmers uncovered a cache of bones that, when assembled, formed a skeleton eight feet in height. The skull's lack of "protruding cheekbones" suggested that it belonged to "a different race of men" than the Native Americans.

As is usually the way when the bones of a giant are discovered, when exposed to air, they quickly disintegrated. Only the skull, which Quickert reports had teeth measuring a full one-inch in length, remained intact. Quickert doesn't reveal the fate of the giant's skull, so keep your eyes open next rummage sale season.

Since the skeleton was assembled by farmers instead of archeologists, it seems wrong to take their estimation of size as accurate. It also seems unlikely that the bones could survive being assembled by laymen but soon after be destroyed by contact with the air. It's much more likely that this was a tall tale Quickert erroneously took as fact.

Quickert supposes the skeleton may have belonged to a people who inhabited "New Iceland" according to the Icelandic sagas. Quickert puts forth the idea that a war erupted between these legendary "Germanic people" and a "Mongolian people"—the Native Americans—which ended in the total destruction of these ancient European giants. Is this hard to believe? Yes, a bit.

Just as the identity of the mound builders are a mystery, so is the purpose of the mounds, though it's now widely accepted that the effigies at Lizard Mound may have been used to indicate a source of fresh water. A large number of the mound shapes represent water spirits, and the park is located above the headwaters of the Milwaukee River and thus is surrounded by numerous springs.

Today, the official count of effigy mounds at Lizard Mound is twenty-eight. The original number of mounds was thought to be sixty or more. The rest of the cluster, like most of Wisconsin's effigy mounds, was destroyed by agricultural practices. Many farmers didn't recognize the earthen mounds for what they were or, possibly, simply didn't care.

Section I: Northern Washington County

Nearly all of the mounds that remain in the park have been disturbed to some extent.

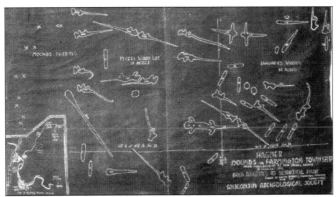

Image courtesy of Washington County Historical Society.

Before the land became a state park in 1950—and later a county park in 1986—the mounds were often invaded by amateur archeologists called "antiquarians." These novice diggers would search through the mounds as a weekend distraction; they were looking for clues to the identity of the mound builders. Because most of these amateurs used little, if any, scientific technique, we'll never know how many bodies were actually buried in the mounds. It's unsettling to think about how many artifacts or human remains were taken as trophies by these well-intentioned grave robbers.

It wasn't until 1960 that an actual professional dig took place. Milwaukee Public Museum anthropologist Lee A. Parsons and several University of Wisconsin-Milwaukee students began an excavation in hopes of finding a burial that might have gone undetected by the antiquarians. The goal was to install a museum-quality in-situ exhibit. This means they wanted to find human remains and build an exhibit over them in their natural position. This could be considered macabre and insensitive in the present day, but one must remember America in 1960 was a much different place.

It only took a few days of excavation for Parsons and crew to uncover human remains in Linear Mound #18. They found the badly decomposed jawbone of an infant and the wonderfully preserved skeleton of a female adult between the ages of twenty-one and thirty-five. The remains of the infant were removed for scientific study, and a concrete and Plexiglas case were built over the partially exposed remains of the female. It's unknown if this was a mother and her child, though they appeared to have been buried at the same time.

Sadly, vandalism was still a problem even after Lizard Mound became a state park. During his dig, Parsons discovered fresh evidence of looting in a nearby water-spirit effigy.

The installation of an exhibit intended to educate the public about the mound builders and the respectful way they treated their dead did nothing to keep troublemakers away. In 1975, the exhibit was smashed open and the woman's bones were strewn about. A nineteen-year-old Waupaca boy stopped by the park for a drink of water and took the woman's skull thinking it belonged to a "monkey." Apparently, he hadn't wondered why broken glass and bones were all around. Having heard about the vandalism and theft and that the skull might be valuable, he turned it over to the Waupaca County Sheriff's Department. One wonders what would have happened had the skull been reported as worthless.

The skull was relatively undamaged. It was returned to the park and reunited with its rightful owner. The exhibit was eventually dismantled, and the much-abused skeleton was reinterred.

All the ingredients for an intense haunting are present at Lizard Mound. That's why I wasn't too surprised when I was contacted by Amy. In the autumn of 1999, she and her family took a nocturnal trip to Lizard Mound after hearing about the park and its legends. They experienced something they'll never forget.

Amy had heard that during full moons and on Friday the Thirteenth, or Halloween, which are all supernaturally significant times, the spirits of the mound builders are particularly capable of protecting the effigies. Oftentimes, these vengeful spirits are joined by a fearsome beast. Here is what she had to say.

> It was in October or November. It wasn't Halloween, but it was near that time, and the moon was full. We had heard the stories about the place. It was me, my [now] ex-husband, three eight-year-olds, a five-year-old, and my eighteen-month-old. [Amy's three children and two of their friends.]
>
> After walking the trail through the park, my ex was showing the kids a circle mound he had heard wouldn't collect leaves or snow.

That's when her former husband decided to see if the legend was true. He tried to provoke the spirits.

He started to make very rude comments, while striking the mound. He threatened to start a fire. It got very cold. Leaves began to blow [across the ground], but the trees were still. There was a noise like many people or things running toward us through the woods—sticks breaking all around us.

I grabbed the kids and started running. I was pushing the stroller while the [other] kids were hanging onto me. We lost my ex, but we could hear him behind us. He was screaming like mad. I was chanting, "Please don't hurt my kids."

As we were running, there were red lights all over the woods. They made a sound like [shooting] arrows. Nothing hit us, but there was a very angry feeling. The noise was so loud, but as soon as we got out of the woods, it stopped.

I realized I lost the keys to the car. My ex went back in [to find them] and the noise started again. He came flying back out and started throwing up.

I asked Amy if she thought the red lights were angry spirits, perhaps the glowing eyes of effigy creatures in physical form.

"I don't know how to interpret the red lights. All I know is that they were there alongside of us, almost ushering us out. They did not touch us, [but] there was noise all around. I was worried about the kids."

The eight-year-olds and the five-year-old remember the noises and the lights. The youngest, now thirteen, still refuses to go to the park even in daytime, though he remembers nothing from that night. The older children recall seeing shadows in the woods resembling people on horseback.

If there is ever a haunting I hope is true, it's this one. After all that's happened to the effigy mounds, the mound builders are justified in protecting what is theirs.

I've been to Lizard Mound County Park many times. All I've experienced is a sense of mystery and wonder, a feeling of peace. My chief memory of the park is watching small whirlwinds dance among the mounds, carrying autumn leaves into the air for a brief moment and then dissipating.

I doubt Amy's ex-husband intended any real harm. He was merely looking for a cheap thrill. Perhaps he felt he should show off for the children. Something at Lizard Mound didn't appreciate his hijinks though, and he learned a serious lesson in respect.

I hope Amy's youngest outgrows his fear of Lizard Mound. I'm convinced if you go there with good intentions, the long-lost mound builders will be more than happy to rest in peace.

Monster near the Mounds

Linda S. Godfrey's outstanding book *Strange Wisconsin: More Badger State Weirdness* contains a creature sighting I found particularly interesting. On November 12, 2006, two men were driving down Shalom Drive, which is off State Highway 144. At about 8:30 p.m., a furry, muscular, deer-sized creature "lumbered" across the road in front of them. They described it as resembling an enormous, tailless wolf. In 2006, there was an outbreak of similar sightings in southeastern Wisconsin, the most famous of which occurred at Holy Hill in Erin (see section 3 of this book). Godfrey attributed these sightings to a creature called "the bearwolf" and noted that sightings of these bizarre canines often occur near sacred Native American land, such as Lizard Mound.

I contacted Linda for advice regarding this Native American connection, and she referred me to another of her books, *Hunting the American Werewolf*. In *Hunting*, Linda points out Native American tribes regard underground springs as particularly potent supernatural locations, which can act as doorways from the spirit world. She also concluded that many of the locations where these strange animals are seen contain water-spirit effigy mounds.

The 2006 Shalom Drive sighting took place barely 2.5 miles from Lizard Mound County Park, a place ornamented with water-spirit effigy mounds that are surrounded by underground springs. On a whim, I looked up the moon's phase for November 12, 2006; it was full. Legend has it that full moons are one of the times when the spirits of Lizard Mound are particularly active. Was this animal actually a water spirit? The next time you're out driving near Lizard Mound on a full-moon night, make sure you brake for bearwolves.

Directions

From Milwaukee: Take HWY 41/45 to West Bend. Exit at HWY 33, and head east.

From Fond du Lac: Take HWY 41 to Allenton. Exit at HWY 33, and head east.

Section I: Northern Washington County

From Madison: Take HWY 151 to Beaver Dam. Exit at HWY 33, and head east.

Once in West Bend: From HWY 33, turn north onto HWY 144 N/N Main Street. Follow HWY 144. Turn right onto CTY A. The entrance to the park is on the right.

Kewaskum: Goat Man Road

About two miles east of Kewaskum is the Milwaukee River Flood Plain Forest. It's 119 acres in size and is part of the Kettle Moraine State Forest. South Mill Road takes you deep into this thickly forested area, where it dead-ends. During summer, the canopy blocks out the light on several areas of the road, leaving it in perpetual shadow. If you ask residents of Kewaskum about South Mill Road, many will give you a confused stare. If, however, you ask about the whereabouts of Goat Man Road, you'll get reliable directions in a flash. The Goat Man is without a doubt Washington County's most bizarre and well known legend.

Too unbelievable to be considered a cryptid, too flesh-and-blood to be a ghost, this creature is often classified as a satyr. Satyrs are benign nature spirits from Greek mythology. These man-goat hybrids, while occasionally depicted as dangerous, were mostly passive-aggressive. They loved wine, women, and song and were always a bit shy. At their worst, they should be considered tricksters and nothing more. *Should* is the key word in that sentence. If the Goat Man of Washington County is a satyr, he isn't passive-aggressive; he's a stone-cold killer. If there's one entity in this book that I hope is just a legend, it's the Goat Man. The stories depict the beast as fierce and downright terrifying. The creature haunts the nightmares of children all over the county and is reputed to frequent at least three locations, the two most famous of which are isolated country roads. What is interesting is there are two very different legends, as well as two very different physical descriptions of the creature (to see what I mean read "Hogsback Road" in section 3).

The Goat Man Road legend centers around an abusive fiend who once lived with his young wife, isolated and alone, in the forest somewhere around the incredibly nonspecific time frame of "a long time ago." The man was utterly loathsome. He hated everyone and everything, including his poor wife, whom he often battered. One night, the violent lout went too far and murdered his wife. But even ending another human's life wasn't enough to satiate his thirst for cruelty. He stumbled out to the pen in back of the house and began beating the goats that he kept. One of the goats managed to gore him with its sharp horns. The brute fell to the ground, and the goats scrambled to freedom. Unable to stop the bleeding and living too deep in the woods to find help, he bled to death somewhere in the forest. A fitting finish for such a nice guy, I say.

Sadly, he somehow returned to the wilderness as a grotesque mockery of his untimely, but much deserved, end. He wanders the woods as the murderous Goat Man, and if the legend is to be believed, he's still looking for more victims. That's a pretty traumatizing campfire tale, right? I figured that was about all it was until I spoke with Washington County resident Jason Miller. Jason claims to have encountered the Goat Man, and he was anything but an amorous, drunken trickster.

In the autumn of 2003, Jason set up his tree stand off South Mill Road in preparation to enjoy some bow hunting. When he returned to hunt a few days later, he discovered it had been taken down and moved about a hundred yards from its original location. There were marks on it that resembled hoofprints.

Thinking it was a combination of another hunter's prank and the marks of some ordinary animal like a deer, Jason put the stand back in the tree. A few weeks later, he again returned. He sat there, hoping to spy a trophy buck. Instead, he saw something entirely unexpected.

The relative quiet of the forest was disturbed by the sounds of something large approaching, something that sounded angry. Looking off into the thick brush, Jason could hardly believe what shambled into the clearing.

"It was the size of a deer, tan and gray in color. It looked like a goat but with a human head and arms. I remember it had a beard that was gray and very long.

"It smelled like rotting flesh and garbage all mixed into one. I remember it was swearing, literally talking under its breath, something about 'trespassers.' What scared me most was the sight of it."

Jason sat in utter shock as he watched the creature, bow at the ready should it notice him in the trees.

Fortunately for Jason, the Goat Man didn't notice him or was looking for a different "trespasser."

"I didn't waste any time getting out of there. I left as soon as he was out of sight. I kept an arrow nocked 'cause I didn't know what else to do, really. I had heard stories about how violent he can get."

Jason once thought nothing of casually entering those woods, but now?

"I don't like going there anymore…especially not without protection." Jason's close encounter with the foul-mouthed satyr is likely to remain with him as long as he lives.

"Eight years later, some of the details are a bit blurry, but I'll never forget what he looked like. I'll never forget."

Directions

From Milwaukee: Take HWY 41/45 to Kewaskum. Turn right onto HWY 28/Main Street.

From Fond du Lac: Take HWY 41/45 to HWY 28. Exit, and follow HWY 28 east to Kewaskum.

From Madison: Take HWY 151 to Beaver Dam. Exit at HWY 33, and head east. Follow HWY 33 east to HWY 45. Take HWY 45 north to Kewaskum. Turn right onto HWY 28/Main Street.

Once in Kewaskum: From HWY 28/Main Street, turn south onto S Mill Road.

Section I: Northern Washington County

West Bend: AmericInn

Most of us have wondered at least once in our lifetime how we'd react if we ever encountered a ghost. When I began writing this book, I wondered that at least once a day. A young woman named Chrystal doesn't need to wonder anymore, not since she met "Henry," the West Bend AmericInn's permanent guest.

Chrystal contacted me online and agreed to meet me at a diner in downtown West Bend to talk about her experience.

When Chrystal started working at the hotel in 2003, she'd been warned about the ghost of an old man who'd died on the second floor, but she never expected to actually see him. The shy blonde's eyes widened as she described her encounter with the supernatural.

"As a housekeeper, I got used to people walking by the rooms, popping their heads in to ask questions. I didn't think much of it when I saw an older man looking into a room I was cleaning. He had white hair with a receding hairline [and was] wearing a white dress shirt and brown dress pants. He carried a brown briefcase and had a suit jacket over his arm. He was just standing outside the doorway beside my [cleaning] cart staring at me. I started toward him and asked if he needed anything for his room. He took a step back and started off down the hall. I went to look for him, and no one was there. There was no way he could have gone into another room without me hearing. The hallways are really long too. In seconds, he was gone."

This wasn't her only encounter with "Henry."

"I was finishing a room on the second floor. When you're a housekeeper, you develop a routine. I always vacuumed last after making the bed. I went out into the hallway to get my vacuum, then when I came back into the room not ten seconds later..." At this point, she shivered involuntarily and rubbed her own arms to warm herself. "The bed was unmade and the impression of a person was on the mattress and pillows. I didn't leave the doorway. No one could have come past me. I started freaking out. I ran downstairs to the lobby. I was so afraid that I was almost in tears. I was begging someone to finish cleaning the room for me, but no one would. I had to reclean the room myself. When I got back there, I chanted over and over, 'I'm so sorry, but I have to make the bed!' It was so horrible making the bed while this invisible person may have still been in it."

I thanked her for sharing such a personal, unmistakably traumatizing experience and then changed the subject to something more mundane. After we said our good-byes, I walked home putting myself in her place the day Henry wanted to take a nap. If it had been me, I'd have told him to make his own bed and then promptly put in an application at the nearest drive-through. Chrystal's a lot braver than she gives herself credit for being.

Directions

From Milwaukee: Take HWY 41/45 to West Bend. Exit at HWY 33, and head west.

From Fond du Lac: Take HWY 41 to Allenton. Exit at HWY 33, and head east.

From Madison: Take HWY 151 to Beaver Dam. Exit at HWY 33, and head east.

Once in West Bend: The hotel is on the north side of HWY 33.

Section I: Northern Washington County

West Bend: Eisenbahn Trail

You're hot and tired. All day you've been washing dishes in a tavern kitchen in the West Bend neighborhood of Barton. Your shift ends in an hour, and the boss is just allowing you your first break of the afternoon. You need distance from the miserable place. You walk as far away as you reasonably can in your allotted fifteen minutes of solitude. Ahead of you, clouds hang heavy and dark. You wonder when it'll rain. Away somewhere in the distance, there's a rumble. Thunder, you assume.

Slowly, it occurs to you the sound is getting nearer, but it's coming from behind you. Then you hear it, low and lonesome—the wail of a train's whistle. You turn and look as a locomotive rockets past you heading toward the storm. It's a very romantic scene, rich with blue-collar metaphor—at least it would be were it not for the fact the tracks had been ripped up and replaced with the asphalt of the Eisenbahn State Trail long ago.

The trail is now used for biking and walking. It begins in southern West Bend, runs through the Kettle Moraine State Forest, and ends twenty-four miles later in the Fond Du Lac County community of Eden.

The Washington County segment of tracks was first built in 1871 by the Chicago and North Western Company. In 1999, the tracks were abandoned, just like in other communities all across America. These days, the rails, once the backbone of America, are primarily used for industry. Communities are littered with mile after mile of these decaying, overgrown remains. Instead of leaving the disposal of these skeletal relics to time and weather, many communities have taken steps to utilize and beautify these tracks. In 2004, the Department of Natural Resources and

Washington County developed and began maintaining the twelve miles of the Eisenbahn in Washington County.

Image courtesy of Washington County Historical Society.

When I first learned of this spectral locomotive, I wondered if perhaps concentrated nostalgia for the glory days of the American railroad had somehow focused itself on this section of track, resulting in this rather unconventional apparition. Little did I know, the most likely source for the haunting was far more tragic than a technology grown obsolete.

My earliest research for the book began close to home. I turned to friends who'd grown up in the county for tips, leads, and advice. I was discussing this book one night with a friend who, like me, has a feverish passion for ghost stories. I began proudly telling her the story of the Barton ghost train, ecstatic to have such a legend in the book. My friend, having lived in West Bend her whole life, thought it old news. *Thanks for telling me about it,* I thought to myself, my feelings a bit hurt that she wasn't as excited as I. Trying to recover, I gave her my half-baked theory for the source of the haunting. She partially stifled a roll of her eyes and politely offered her own theory.

The Little Girl Lost

For pedestrians, the rails were often the quickest path between two points, especially when the Milwaukee River stood between you and your destinations. In the Barton area of West Bend, people often took the railroad trestle as a shortcut despite the obvious danger involved. Now a paved portion of the Eisenbahn, in the 1950s, it was only track with a shallow river beneath.

The community's children were especially unfazed by the peril involved in taking this shortcut. One day, two little girls hurrying home from school were running across it. Somehow, one of the girls became stuck in the tracks. In the distance came the scream of a train's whistle. The train pressed down on the girls. The engineer couldn't stop in time. One of them ran to safety; the other one was killed. Since that day, people have seen a little girl's apparition running across the trestle, still on her way home from school. My friend believes it no coincidence that the apparition of a train is spotted along that same stretch of tracks.

It is said that traumatic events can leave lasting impressions on the environment in which they occurred. Perhaps that train will always be traveling down those tracks just as that little girl will always be running for home. Months went by, and I moved on in my research. I'd not thought about the Eisenbahn Trail and its tragic haunting for a long time when a lengthy, anonymous e-mail arrived in my inbox. What follows is a rewritten account of genuine experiences. Though I've made a few edits for clarity's sake, all details involving the paranormal have been unaltered. It is important to note the wooden bridge where this story takes place isn't the trestle where the little girl was killed, but a one-lane bridge on Woodford Road, which crosses over what is now the Eisenbahn, not far from it. All names in this story have been changed to protect those involved.

The Gate Incident

It all started in the summer of 2000. My younger sister Alexis's flamboyant boyfriend, Mike, was visiting from Michigan, along with his friend John. They were hanging out with me and my boyfriend, Sam, and our friends Kyle and Missy. We were all still high school students then.

We walked from Missy's house up to the wooden bridge that went over the railroad tracks where we'd hang out.

Missy told us about the little girl's ghost on the trestle farther down the tracks. Nearly everyone in the group quickly agreed that they felt the presence of a little girl who was happy to have visitors, people she could play with. As the sun began to set, the feeling changed from playfulness to dread and urgency. Alexis began shouting for us to run back to Missy's house.

Back at the house, Kyle seemed to fixate on the window facing the bridge. When I turned to look at the bridge as well, it felt like something was pushing against me with great force. Wanting to get as far away from that place as possible, we drove back to my place, taking the long way so as to avoid driving over that bridge.

Later, Kyle told me that as he was staring out the window, he plainly saw three figures staring back at him from the bridge. One was a woman with no legs; the second was a man with a missing left hand. The third was a dark, shadowy figure.

He felt that the little girl had sent us away as these others spirits approached. Soon, the rest opened up and told what they had felt, seen, or heard. Alexis described seeing a gate of light open on the bridge and a pair of black eyes exiting from it.

Even though we were scared, we visited the bridge several more times that summer to try to understand what had happened. After one visit, I started playing hopscotch, and I didn't know why. On another trip, we brought a video camera and had footage of what resembled a little girl floating above the bridge, but Kyle's dad thought it was a blank and recorded over it. Soon, it felt as though spirits were following us home. Alexis started having visions of a lonely grave beside an evergreen tree, marked only by a white stone with no inscription.

Eventually, Alexis and I told our parents. Mom told us to ignore it all, pretend it didn't exist, and stay away from the bridge. If we didn't involve ourselves, and if we didn't pay attention to whatever it was, it would lose interest in us. Our group decided we'd never talk about it again.

A year passed, but I still couldn't stop thinking about "the gate incident," as our group called it. I had to talk with someone, so I confided in my friend Jackie. When I told her of Alexis's visions, Jackie said it reminded her of a small cemetery in the vicinity of the bridge. She insisted we investigate.

I reluctantly drove us to the cemetery, arriving just before sunset. Jackie led me to an evergreen. Sure enough, there was a white stone lacking an inscription. I immediately felt as if I'd made a huge mistake. I wanted to leave. Jackie ignored me and knelt down by the stone as I continued to demand we go. Jackie stood up. With her back to me, she began to play hopscotch just as I inexplicably had once before. I was terrified. I managed to squeak out, "Jackie?"

"This is my body now, and I want to play!" she turned to face me with a twisted mockery of a childish expression.

Light was fading quickly as Jackie began to play hopscotch again. I pleaded with this "little girl" to leave my friend, even promising that we'd come back tomorrow and play even more. She turned and said in a voice that wasn't Jackie's, "Do you promise?" I promised, and at that moment, Jackie returned in a daze, her facial expressions and voice her own once more. I screamed at her to run to my car and not to look back.

As we sped from the cemetery, Jackie kept asking me what had happened. She remembered kneeling down beside a stone and then feeling as if she were looking at a film negative of the world. Then she'd heard me imploring her to run. When I told her what happened, she became horrified.

I don't know what possessed Jackie, but it was no little girl. Could it have been one of the other spirits my friends saw or those black eyes? I told Alexis and the others about what had happened, so that they'd never find themselves anywhere near the grave in that little cemetery.

The events of that summer still confuse me. I don't know what that "gate" was or why this thing wanted to possess us. I did learn a lesson though. Be careful when communicating with something you don't understand. Sometimes, what seems innocent and playful can be something else entirely.

Directions

From Milwaukee: Take 41/45 to West Bend. Exit at HWY 33, and head east.

From Fond du Lac: Take 41 to Allenton. Exit at HWY 33, and head east.

From Madison: Take HWY 151 to Beaver Dam. Exit at HWY 33, and head east.

Once in West Bend: From HWY 33, turn north onto HWY 144 N/N Main Street. Follow HWY 144. Turn left onto Salisbury Road. Turn left onto Hi Mt. Road, which turns into Northwestern Avenue and park. Walk northwest along the trail. The first bridge where the little girl is seen crosses the Milwaukee River and River Drive; the second bridge, where the possession took place, passes over the Eisenbahn Trail.

West Bend: Healing Elements Day Spa

Experiencing the paranormal can make you question your own sanity. Just ask Nicolette Kearns, owner of Healing Elements Day Spa. She and her staff have been subjected to unexplainable phenomena on a regular basis since the spa opened in 2008.

After Nicolette called and gave me a description of what was happening at her business, she asked if I knew of any paranormal investigators who could come in and reassure her and the rest of Healing Elements that they had a firm grasp on reality. I explained that I had joined a group called the Paranormal Investigation and Research Society (PIRS) as part of the writing process, and we'd be more than happy to come in and conduct an investigation.

The team arrived just after dark in early December. Nicolette gave us a tour of the building, along with a long list of ghostly happenings.

In the hair salon, an employee was hit in the back of the head with a plastic bead while styling a client's hair. No one else was there, and no one was wearing beads. In the nail salon, both staff and clients had heard the disembodied laughter of children. A staff member was shoved at the hips by something unseen in an employee area. On another occasion, a few feet away, Nicolette and an employee were folding towels when the clothes dryer door opened and closed under its own power. Nicolette was also witness to two other dramatic occurrences, both of which happened while she was giving massages. The first occurred in the "Fire Room." She watched as a client's robe, which hung from a hook on the wall, was lifted up in the air by an unseen force and then slowly lowered back down. The second incident happened in the "Earth Room." A tall, black, shadowy figure, described as "male," appeared and then disappeared in her peripheral vision.

We asked if there was a known reason for the haunting. A local psychic had told Nicolette that the building was located on Native American "ritual ground." In addition, a client who claimed to be clairvoyant asserted the building contained a "portal." Armed with this information, the group blanketed the building with cameras and began the investigation.

I was the first to investigate the Earth Room, along with Nicolette and fellow PIRS-er, Walter Skilling. Minutes into the investigation, our walkie-talkies began picking up a strong static interference. We tried switching channels and powering the radio on and off, but nothing helped. We ended up having to shut it off. Later that night, two other PIRS teams had the exact same interference happen in the Earth Room. This occurred nowhere else in the building.

Strange patches of energy about six feet off the ground were detected in various portions of the lobby and hair salon using K-II electromagnetic field (EMF) detectors. We couldn't determine a source for this energy. The most common cause of high EMF readings is old wiring or cheaply made appliances leaking electricity into the atmosphere. None of the energy was located near an appliance or outlet. It should be noted that the building had some of the best wiring of any PIRS has investigated. Almost no EMF leaks were found. Our detectors nearly had to physically touch an outlet or breaker box to register an energy spike.

Two PIRS members reported seeing a green glow of light in two different locations in the spa. Both times, the light disappeared before the source could be determined. I also got inexplicably sick to my stomach in the employee area of the spa, near where the dryer door was seen to open and close on its own.

After a few hours had passed, we packed up our gear and went home to review hours of evidence. Frustratingly enough, we didn't record anything anomalous on video or audio.

I stopped by the Washington County Historical Society to try to figure out if the spa's land held any particular significance to Native Americans. In 1983, a Native American burial had been excavated about a mile from the spa near the intersection of Paradise Drive and US Highway 45 by Lynne Goldstein of the University of Wisconsin-Milwaukee. However, this was an isolated burial—as opposed to an entire burial ground—so it doesn't necessarily mean the spa is on ancient "ritual ground."

While we didn't capture any physical evidence, there had been plenty of personal experiences and we documented that there was some unexplainable energy there. Does the spa conceal a portal to the other side? That we can't say. I think Nicolette and her staff now have a bit more confidence in their own sanity, though. Perhaps next time, I'll stop in for a massage in the Fire Room and declare it research.

Directions

From Milwaukee: Take HWY 41/45 to West Bend. Exit at Paradise Road, and head west.

From Fond du Lac: Take HWY 41 to Allenton. Exit at HWY 33, and head east to HWY 45. Take HWY 45 south to Paradise Road. Exit at Paradise Road, and head west.

From Madison: Take HWY 151 to Beaver Dam. Exit at HWY 33, and head east to HWY 45. Take HWY 45 south to Paradise Road. Exit at Paradise Road, and head west.

Once in West Bend: From Paradise Road, turn south onto Continental Drive. The spa is on the right.

Section I: Northern Washington County

West Bend: Kettle Moraine YMCA Farmhouse

The following story is based entirely on an e-mail sent to me by a West Bend resident who wishes to remain anonymous. I have edited and rewritten the e-mail, but none of the facts have been altered.

I rented a house at 1035 Cedar Street from the Kettle Moraine YMCA. The white two-story was built in 1900 as a single-family home and was nicknamed "The Farmhouse" by the YMCA for the fact that it was once the lone dwelling on a side of the main drag that was farmland.

In early 2007, my mom told me that the lower unit of the house was available for a very affordable price. Once I moved in, I began hearing the occasional thumps or footsteps, but there would be plenty of odd sounds. That's just a part of living in an old house. Soon, I began hearing what sounded like a bowling ball being dropped onto the floor above. This sound would happen once or twice a week, usually late at night. The upstairs renter often worked third shift, and aside from stopping home for lunch around midnight, he would be gone all night. The first few times I heard the noise, I looked for his truck in the driveway, but it was gone. I met him later, and he asked how things were going. I told him about the noises. He laughed and said it was just the ghost. "You'll get used to it," he added.

A friend and his girlfriend were visiting one evening. No sooner had he asked where that "bowling ball noise" was than *boom*! The walls rattled, the light fixture swayed, and he was out of his seat and out the front door in a hurry.

The noises upstairs continued. On several occasions, I heard a muffled conversation. I could never make out the words. One day, what sounded like a woman began humming a tune like an old radio jingle. I wanted to pinch myself because I knew there was no one up there.

Then I began to see things. From my living room couch, I would occasionally glimpse a shadowy cat shape in the kitchen. When I'd turn my head, it would fade away or slink down the hallway. I had a strong feeling of sadness for the creature... I believed it was something that had been loved and just wanted to share my space for a little while. I hope it knew that it was welcome to sit in the room whenever it liked. My collie would occasionally look up from his nap and stare at the spot where it most often appeared.

Eventually, the renter upstairs decided he had had enough and moved out. Apparently, whatever was upstairs was much more active than what I dealt with. Soon after, the Y decided not to rent the upper unit and boarded up the door to the stairs. Imagine my surprise when I distinctly heard kids running up and down the stairs. There was no way in, and the blocked door was undisturbed.

When a fuse would blow, I would have to make a trip into the narrow dirt-floor cellar. It was an area that no one would go into willingly. The Y's maintenance guy refused to go down there by himself. I used to have nightmares about something living down there. In my dreams, I would see a white staircase that somehow replaced the dirty cellar steps. I'd push the flimsy wooden door open carefully, and though I could never see it, I knew a thin man with stark-white skin was hiding behind the door. His mouth would open in a grotesque yawn, and I would wake up. The nightmare never changed.

The strangest thing ever to happen to me at the house occurred early one morning. Around 4:30 a.m., I was sitting on my couch tying my shoes, the television playing in the background. I looked up at the screen, and the "Program Keyword Search" box opened on the screen. The cursor spelled out "Civil War." A list of programs came up, and the cursor moved down to record a show. I found the remote sitting on the back of the couch, untouched by human hands. I admit that there is a chance someone else nearby had the same remote, but it was the eeriest experience.

More people began telling me about the weirdness that surrounded the house. An old man who grew up near the house told me one morning he and some other kids were walking to school—sometime in the 1960s—and saw that the house was wide open, the doors, windows, everything. One kid walked up to the front door to look inside and found it was empty. The family had evidently packed up overnight and left. Neighborhood kids started calling it "the haunted house" and dared each other to walk all the way through.

    A neighbor who rented another of the Y's houses told me that her friend was a psychic medium and hated looking at my house. She, too, said that there was a very bad energy up in the attic window. After I had moved out, my mom remarked that she never liked to look up at the attic window. She said it felt like someone was staring at her, a man with a large forehead, like a physical defect. The old place was eventually razed for the Y's parking lot expansion in 2009. I still can't fully grasp what was going on inside the walls of that farmhouse.

Directions

From Milwaukee: Take HWY 41/45 to West Bend. Exit at HWY 33, and head east.

From Fond du Lac: Take HWY 41 to Allenton. Exit at HWY 33, and head east.

From Madison: Take HWY 151 to Beaver Dam. Exit at HWY 33, and head east.

Once in West Bend: The YMCA is on the south side of HWY 33.
Important notice: The house is no longer standing. The space it once occupied is now a parking lot.

West Bend: Newark Cemetery

On August 1, 1855, a murder known as one of the most diabolical in the history of Wisconsin occurred outside of West Bend in the town of Trenton. While this murder, or any murder for that matter, is a wicked deed, the savage lynching it brought about was ten times as appalling and is one of the most brutal examples of mob justice in American history.

What follows is an oversimplified, brief summary of an alleged crime and the subsequent lynching. The entire affair is very complex and involves politics, xenophobia, cronyism, and anti-Catholicism. To get the true historical context, I suggest you read the book *Dark Lanterns: An American Lynching* by Jack H. Anderson, which is where I culled the following information.

A twenty-year-old man named George De Bar visited John Muehr's farm in the middle of the night. Muehr owed De Bar a small sum of money for work he'd done on his farm.

These are the facts according to John Muehr: De Bar asked for water. Muehr offered him a beer and went into the cellar. He returned with De Bar's drink only to be hit over the head with a hammerlike weapon. De Bar then allegedly chased Mrs. Muehr and cut her throat several times until she dropped to the ground from loss of blood. De Bar also supposedly attacked a fourteen-year-old hired boy named Paul Winderling, who'd awoken during the attacks. Paul was stabbed through the throat and killed. During the attacks on his wife and hired hand, John Muehr escaped and ran into the night screaming, "Murder!"

When help arrived, the Muehr's shanty-house was found burned to the ground and Winderling's partially burned body had been dragged near the rubble. Mrs. Muehr had recovered and was found in hiding. De Bar was gone.

De Bar was arrested the next day in Milwaukee. As he was transported back to West Bend, he allegedly confessed to his guards that he'd gone to the farm with the intent to kill Muehr in retaliation for his alleged attack with a club at Trenton's polling place the previous spring.

Of the recent attacks, De Bar said he recalled seeing Mrs. Muehr holding a candle after he'd struck John Muehr. He tried to wrestle it from her but remembers nothing of slashing her, killing the boy, or burning down the house.

De Bar was an American-born citizen in a community mostly comprised of German immigrants. At the time, the anti-immigrant/anti-Catholic American Party warned that the latest wave of immigrants, mostly Irish and German Catholics, were taking jobs from "native"—meaning native-born—Americans, with their willingness to work for low wages. The party also warned that the pope would soon hold sway over American politicians because of this influx of Catholics. While De Bar's political affiliation is unknown, this could explain why Muehr had attacked him at a polling place, if he truly did. It should be mentioned that De Bar was wearing a style of hat associated with the American Party the night of the attacks.

The people of West Bend were outraged and wanted the death of De Bar. They feared this "native" who'd murdered a German would escape justice, so they decided they needed to take matters into their own hands. On August 8, De Bar entered a plea of not guilty at the original Washington County Courthouse—a wooden structure that was replaced in 1889 by what is now called the Old Courthouse Museum.

As he was escorted from the building, he and his guards were swarmed by a screaming mob that numbered to the hundreds. De Bar was knocked to the ground and beaten. The militias from Milwaukee and Port Washington, called to protect De Bar, only spectated, except for those who joined the mob. Eventually, the crowd dropped a tree stump weighting over a 150 pounds on De Bar's head. From there, he was stripped naked, dragged, and beaten all through town until they reached the Milwaukee River alongside present-day Washington Street. There, they strung him up by his ankles. When it was noticed he was still breathing, the mob cut him down and then hanged him by the neck instead. With that, the crowd was satisfied. Justice had been served as far as they were concerned. No one was ever convicted for De Bar's murder, which, in my opinion, was even more heinous than the crime he was accused of committing.

According to stories whispered in present-day West Bend, De Bar was supposedly buried in an unmarked gave under a tree along the borders of Newark Cemetery in the Barton area of West Bend, though the location of his burial was apparently never recorded.

Despite the sensational and gruesome nature of the Winderling murder and De Bar's lynching, to my knowledge, there isn't a single ghost story surrounding the events of the summer of 1855. Perhaps no ghost is needed when the acts of men are haunting enough.

Directions

From Milwaukee: Take HWY 41/45 to West Bend. Exit at CTY D, and head east.

From Fond du Lac: Take HWY 41 south. Exit at CTY D, and follow CTY D east.

From Madison: Take HWY 151 to Beaver Dam. Exit at HWY 33, and head east to HWY 45. Take HWY 45 north to CTY D. Exit at CTY D, and head east.

In West Bend: From CTY D, turn north onto Lighthouse Lane. Turn right onto Newark Drive. The cemetery is on the left.

Section I: Northern Washington County

West Bend: Old Courthouse Museum

The old Washington County courthouse dominates the landscape of West Bend. Standing eight stories high, this gorgeous example of Richardsonian Romanesque architecture is the tallest building in the city. In fact, the top of its tower is the second highest point in the whole county, second only to Holy Hill Basilica in Erin (see section 3).

For nearly three-quarters of a century, the building hosted courtroom dramas ranging from mundane crimes, such as unlawful cohabitation, to sensational rapes, murders, and attempted suicides. Nowadays, the building is home to the Washington County Historical Society and functions as both a research center and a museum.

For decades, unsettling stories have been whispered around West Bend regarding the old courthouse and the haunting that supposedly occurs there. If anything, the society has embraced the building's supernatural reputation. In 2011, it began offering nighttime "Haunted Museums Tours," and their yearly Halloween fundraiser is consistently their most popular annual event.

The most commonly accused culprit behind the building's reputed haunting is a former custodian known only as "George," who was supposedly killed by lightning while walking between the old courthouse and the Old Sheriff's Residence and Jail, which is located a few yards away on the same property.

I decided to ask WCHS Curator of Education Jessica Sawinski Couch about the legend of George and his lingering presence—not only because she designed the new Haunted Museums Tours but also because she's my wife. It's hard to avoid the questions of a nosy paranormal researcher when you have to eat dinner with him every night. So, is there any truth to either legend? Yes and no. According to Jessica, no evidence has ever been found to support the legend; however, unexplainable phenomena happen on a regular basis in the museum.

George has been seen on at least one occasion. One afternoon in the early 2000s, a volunteer was working at the front desk when she suddenly sensed a presence. She glanced up and saw an unfamiliar man standing by the front door in a blue jumpsuit; he was wearing a large ring of keys at his hip. From across the room, she asked if she could help him. Apparently unaware of her or her inquiry, he turned, walked into the basement stairwell, and never came back out.

A couple of years following that sighting, a former curator went down that same stairwell to use the men's room. A moment later, he came running up the stairs in a fright. All anyone could coax from him was that the incident involved the building's ghost. While it's pure conjecture, one can assume he met George on his appointed rounds. That curator never used the basement men's room again.

George's supposedly electrifying death also leads volunteers to attribute the museum's bizarre lighting problems to the late janitor. All exhibit spaces in the museum use motion-activated lighting. These lights turn on all the time when no one is present. I myself have seen them turn on several times in the middle of the night while walking past the seemingly empty building. The county has had electricians in on several occasions to try to solve the problem, but so far, no one has been able to determine why this occurs. It should be noted that I spent a lot of time at the museum during the summer and autumn of 2011 as a volunteer and as a researcher. In July, the lights exhibited none of their bizarre behavior. But as the months progressed, the phenomena became undeniable. By the time Halloween arrived, the lights were turning on and off constantly on all three floors of the building. Was it just a coincidence? Well, perhaps. But you have to admit, it is rather uncanny.

Another hot spot of activity is the front staircase. The society's executive director, Patricia Lutz, had a run-in with a possible entity in 2011, just a couple of weeks after accepting her position. The event happened on a Monday when the museum was closed to the public, and only she and one other staff member were in the building. She was walking alone from her office to the research center, both of which were located on the third floor, when she saw a "black, shadowy mass" the size of a person float down the front staircase from the corner of her eye. She quickly turned to investigate, only to find herself alone, wondering what exactly she had just seen.

Image courtesy of **Washington County Historical Society.**

Not long after this, a research center volunteer told me of several instances when he was sure he'd heard someone walk up the noisy wooden stairs when he should have been the only person in the building. On a certain Saturday morning, he was so sure someone else was in the building with him that he searched the entire museum but found no one.

A museum patron also e-mailed me her own experience on those same stairs. A young woman named Kristol had brought her family to the society's 2008 Halloween event. Kristol, her husband, and their two young daughters had participated in activities in the courtroom on the second floor. As they were descending the stairs, she noticed a "white cloud" near the bottom of the flight leading to the first floor. She stopped in her tracks and watched as this "cloud" elongated into a smoky ribbon and floated vertically around the chandelier. From there, it snaked its way upward along the outside of the staircase until it disappeared from her sight in transit to the second floor. While the children didn't seem to notice, her husband saw the mysterious vapor as well. He and Kristol grabbed the kids and ran down the remaining steps two at a time. Kristol is convinced it wasn't smoke, as it seemed to exhibit intelligence.

When I asked around the society if it might have been smoke or fog from a Halloween prop, I was told it couldn't have been. The building's smoke alarms are extremely sensitive and have been set off by a single steam tray used during an event. Any sort of flame or artificial fog would set them off almost instantly.

Since no one, including me, had been able to find any record of a man named George working as a custodian at the courthouse, or of someone dying there from a lightning strike, I concluded, just as the society had, that George was merely a legend. Then, one fateful night, just before this book was to be published, a possible answer materialized out of the ether.

In order to finance the book's publication, I began guiding a ghost walk of downtown West Bend based on my research, imaginatively titled "The Downtown West Bend Ghost Walk."

I know you're likely thinking, *He should be in marketing*, right?

Anyway, as we stood in front of the old courthouse, I discovered that the legend of George is based in truth. A patron by the name of Robert Bernhagan offered that his great uncle Waldemar Bernhagan had once been a custodian at the courthouse and presented me with a clipping of his obituary from a West Bend newspaper, marked "June 1938" in pen.

According to the article, Waldemar often used the basement as a "headquarters" to paint and sketch when he'd have a spare moment. On June 30, 1938, Waldemar was sitting in a chair in the basement during an electrical storm when a bolt of lightning struck the building, traveled into the basement, and knocked the thirty-seven-year-old man to the floor. He passed away in Old St. Joseph's Hospital on June 10, 1939, after a "prolonged illness," which was the result of the lightning strike.

Not only was the legend of George largely true, but it was exceptionally exciting to learn the eventually deadly incident had occurred in the basement, an area where the apparition of a custodian has been seen.

The good news is if Waldemar is really the museum's ghost, he seems benign. The ghost makes noise and plays with lights, but mostly, he keeps to himself. It's the curators you have to watch out for. My wife has a nasty right hook if you attempt to touch the artifacts. Trust me, I know.

Section I: Northern Washington County

Death from the Tower

While George, now rightfully identified as Waldemar, is the building's most famous ghost, there is another, more morbid legend circulating on the Internet. The legend claims a young man hanged himself from the courthouse's tower and now his ghost lingers in the building, moving objects, making noise, and occasionally appearing as a dreadful cadaver swinging from the site of his self-facilitated demise.

I asked the Washington County Historical Society about this, and they've found no evidence to support an incident as dramatic and memorable as a suicide from the highest point in the city, nor has anyone ever seen a ghost hanging from the tower. In fact, no evidence has been found of anyone ever dying on the property. Of course, events do have a way of being forgotten over time, the case of Waldemar Bernhagan being an exceptional example. While it's unlikely the actual event happened in such a grandiose manner, there could be some truth to the story, but for now, it remains just a legend.

Directions

From Milwaukee: Take HWY 41/45 to West Bend. Exit at HWY 33, and head east.

From Fond du Lac: Take HWY 41 to Allenton. Exit at HWY 33, and head east.

From Madison: Take HWY 151 to Beaver Dam. Exit at HWY 33, and head east.

Once in West Bend: From HWY 33, turn south onto Seventh Avenue. Turn left onto Chestnut Street. Turn left onto Fifth Avenue. The museum is on the left.

West Bend: Old Sheriff's Residence and Jail

In 2011, the old Washington County Jail, now a museum officially known as the Old Sheriff's Residence and Jail, celebrated its quasquicentennial. To put it more plainly, it turned 125 years old. To celebrate this anniversary, the Washington County Historical Society created a new tour, the "Haunted Museums Tour" (mentioned in "Old Courthouse Museum"). Over the years, staff, volunteers, and visitors alike have had eerie experiences. Unexplained voices, moving objects, and sightings of apparitions have been the norm.

As soon as I learned about these tours, I knew that I wanted to be a part of them. I quickly volunteered as a guide. Not only would it help me research the book, but it was in this building that I had one of my first paranormal experiences.

In 2009, a group of paranormal investigators were conducting an overnight investigation of the jail. My wife, Jessica, who works for the society, was elected to be the staff member on duty. Not wanting to spend the night in a haunted jailhouse with a group of relative strangers, she asked if I'd like to come along as a volunteer and keep her company. I cheerfully agreed. It sounded far more exciting than sitting home alone.

To our surprise, we were invited along on an EVP session in one of the upstairs bedrooms. "EVP" stands for "electronic voice phenomena." This is when audio-recording devices are used to capture sounds not heard by the human ear.

Three investigators, Jessica, and I sat in a semicircle on the bedroom floor asking questions to any spirits that might have been present. While sitting there, I felt a faint sensation of static electricity on my right hand, which was resting on the floor. I looked down and saw the hairs on my

Section I: Northern Washington County

arm standing up. As I told the others, the sensation left me. I raised my hand several inches and found the strange sensation again. The energy continued to drift up and away, over a cradle filled with antique dolls, and then across the room. We eventually lost it a couple of feet from the window. While no physical evidence was captured by any of the group's equipment, never before, or since, have I experienced anything like it.

Since that day, I've spent countless hours as a volunteer in the Old Sheriff's Residence and Jail and not experienced anything remotely paranormal. I'd begun to write off the event as overactive imaginations until July 13, 2011, the night of the inaugural Haunted Museums Tour.

It was nearly 9:00 p.m., and the tour was nearing its end. The group consisted of ten patrons, another guide, and me. As the group was going down into the basement, there suddenly was a loud, rhythmic sound in the cellblock. The sound got nearer and traveled past me, down the stairs, into the basement. To my ear, it sounded somewhat like a baseball card in a bicycle's spokes. Afterward, a patron described it as sounding like "metal coat buttons clicking against a grocery cart." At the time, I thought someone had fallen down the staircase. I called down to the other guide to see if everyone was alright, and she had no clue what I was talking about. As it turns out, only half of us had heard the sound at all. A woman in the basement heard the noise travel loudly past her and then seemingly change directions and go into the furnace room. Her twenty-something-year-old daughter, who was standing right beside her, didn't hear it at all.

The event stands out as exceptional for two reasons. First, only half of us heard the resounding noise. Second, the sound seemed to travel between floors, change directions, and travel into the furnace room, a room long rumored to be the source of the building's haunting and our final stop on the tour.

A legend circulated throughout the community for many years attributes the haunting to a murderous sheriff. This unidentified lawman became so enraged with an unruly inmate that he began beating him. Lost in a fit of violent fury, the sheriff didn't stop until the inmate had been murdered. To hide his horrendous crime, he dragged the lifeless corpse out of the cellblock and then downstairs to the basement where he buried it. The sheriff would have followed the same exact path as the mysterious commotion only half of us had heard.

The next day, I received the following e-mail from one of the patrons, Michele W. She shared with me her twelve-year-old son Spencer's personal experience.

Spencer and I were the last to come out of the [furnace] room last night. As we walked down the hall to catch up to the group, he suddenly shouted out. I turned to him and kinda gave him "the look" for shouting.

On the way home, he told me that when we were in the furnace room, he felt like he had bumped into a spiderweb. He said the sensation came back several times—each time he brushed his arm. As he walked out of the room and started down the hall, the sensation returned much stronger, like someone had pulled on his arm. That was why he had suddenly turned and shouted out—probably why he had a spooked look on his face when I turned to him!

Needless to say, it was an impressive first tour. The historical society is quick to point out that the legend of the murderous sheriff is likely just that, a legend. No evidence of a murder at the old jail, or any death for that matter, has been discovered.

But if there's not a body hidden in the basement of the jail, what tugged on Spencer's arm? That's tough to say. The old jail is largely made of limestone and sits atop a hill largely comprised of limestone. Some paranormal investigators theorize that because limestone primarily consists of organic matter, the stone can be a conduit for a haunting. Some investigators believe that as the organic matter in the stone breaks down, it emits high levels of energy, which can help ghosts to manifest. But if the limestone is helping a spirit manifest, where did the spirit come from in the first place?

No matter what the cause of the unexplainable phenomena at the old jail, thanks to the ongoing efforts of the Washington County Historical Society, people will be able to continue to enjoy its history and its legends for years to come.

Bizarre Fact #1

While no one has ever died at the old jail, one rather gruesome event is remembered by Mrs. Edward Detuncq, daughter of former Washington County Sheriff Adam Held, in the book *The Spirit of West Bend*, by Dorothy E. Williams.

One winter, a man walking from Milwaukee to West Bend went to sleep in a farmer's barn somewhere near the city. When he awoke, his legs were frozen solid. Upon being discovered, he was brought to the jail where a doctor sawed off both his legs with no anesthetic. "He yelled and yelled, not from the pain, but from the thought of being legless," Mrs. Detuncq recalled. He healed at the jail, rolling around the building on a dolly someone had built for him until he was well enough to be sent back to Milwaukee.

Image courtesy of Washington County Historical Society.

Bizarre Fact #2

The Old Sheriff's Residence and Jail has been a filming location for various movies and television programs throughout the years, including the 1999 film adaptation of Michael Lesy's infamous book *Wisconsin Death Trip*. The book chronicles years of madness, murder, and vandalism in the West Central Wisconsin town of Black River Falls during the late nineteenth century.

The old jail was also considered as a filming location for the 2009 film *Public Enemies*, starring Johnny Depp as notorious gangster John Dillinger. When a location scout visited the jailhouse in 2008, the upstairs toilet flushed on its own four times over the course of nearly as many minutes. When the concerned scout asked what was going on, a staff member remarked, "That's just one of our ghosts," not knowing what else to say. Shortly before filming began, a jail in Indiana that Dillinger actually escaped from became available, keeping Johnny away from West Bend. At least, that's the official story.

Directions

From Milwaukee: Take HWY 41/45 to West Bend. Exit at HWY 33, and head east.

From Fond du Lac: Take HWY 41 to Allenton. Exit at HWY 33, and head east.

From Madison: Take HWY 151 to Beaver Dam. Exit at HWY 33, and head east.

Once in West Bend: From HWY 33, turn south onto Seventh Avenue. Turn left onto Chestnut Street. Turn left onto Fifth Avenue. The museum is on the left.

Section I: Northern Washington County

West Bend:
Old St. Joseph's Community Hospital

There once was a time when hospitals weren't just big businesses. There was a time, now nearly forgotten, when hospitals were operated almost exclusively by religious organizations. Such was the case in 1930 when St. Joseph's opened in West Bend.

The Sisters of the Divine Savior nursed, cleaned, and cooked. They did everything short of performing surgeries at old St. Joe's. During the Great Depression, when patients couldn't afford to pay their bills, the sisters gladly accepted food as payment.

Many of these selfless women spent decades laboring at the hospital for the benefit of the community. Sister Cypriana Loessl spent thirty-nine years working in the laundry room until her retirement. Many of them, such as Sister Othilde Thimmel, spent their entire lives nursing the sick of West Bend.

In 1971, the sisters sold ownership of the hospital, and an era ended. In 2000, a new hospital was built outside of West Bend near Washington County Fair Park. These days, the old hospital campus houses St. Joseph's Kraemer Cancer Center and the Albrecht Free Clinic. While St. Joseph's has basically moved away, legend has it that at least one of the sisters stayed behind at the old campus.

Night watchmen report seeing the apparition of a nun strolling around the upper floors of the building, especially the third, where the sisters' quarters was located during the 1930s. Back when the hospital was still there, nurses complained of shadowy figures and the sensation of being followed. I spoke to one woman who used to work in the old hospital, and she informed me that seeing the apparition of a ghostly nun was so common that it was considered a rite of passage for employees. The old hospital is located along my nightly jogging route. When I pass by, I like to imagine one of the sisters is still roaming the old building, looking for someone in need of care. That's an especially heartening thought for someone as prone to twist their knee as I am.

Directions

From Milwaukee: Take HWY 41/45 to West Bend. Exit at HWY 33, and head east.

From Fond du Lac: Take HWY 41 to Allenton. Exit at HWY 33, and head east.

From Madison: Take HWY 151 to Beaver Dam. Exit at HWY 33, and head east.

In West Bend: From HWY 33, turn south onto Eighteenth Avenue. Turn left onto Oak Street. The old hospital is to the left on the corner of Oak and Ridge.

Section I: Northern Washington County

West Bend: Old City Hall

For more than ninety years, the building at 100 North Sixth Avenue was West Bend City Hall. Constructed in 1900, the building not only contained the city's finest assortment of bureaucrats but also the fire department for the first four decades or so. This is why the building looks so distinct. The large tower on the southwest corner of the building was used to dry fire hoses.

If the hoses weren't hung out to dry immediately after use, water residue could seriously damage them. After returning from a call, the daring men of the West Bend Fire Department would have to haul the fifteen-foot-long, heavy, treacherous hoses hand over hand onto a large wooden rack capable of holding 1500 feet of hose. This historical fact is the basis for the legend surrounding Old City Hall, which since the early 1990s, has been used as office space.

In the last couple of decades, rumor has spread that a young fireman met his fate while hoisting his hose—his fire hose of course. One afternoon, the rack gave way while two firemen were attempting to hang several of the hoses. One of the men was crushed to death, and, if the testimony of several people is correct, his ghost is still there.

Mother and son Vickie and Nick Schmidt are two of those people. They worked in the building as custodians from 2001 to 2002. Their opinion? Haunted.

Nick best remembers an overwhelming sense of being watched, no matter where he was in the building—so much so that he regularly would "freak out" and have to hurry from the building.

Vickie says the ghost did a bit more than observe her. On a nightly basis, she'd feel a man's hand tenderly caress her face, as if moving her hair aside. Whatever it was also enjoyed pranking her, particularly when it was time to clean the men's room. Frequently, she'd hear the stall doors lock from the inside as soon as she'd enter the room.

She took all of this in stride until one night when she came to work very ill. The activity was at an all-time high. Doors were locking, faucets turning on and off, and finally, she screamed out, "Quit messing with me! I'm sick!" The rest of the night was quiet.

"For three weeks after that, nothing happened. I sort of missed whatever it was. I said out loud, 'It's okay. I'm not sick anymore; you can go back to doing what you want,' and zing! All the bathrooms started locking again." Vickie said.

Carla W. worked in the building for fifteen years, from 1994 to 2007, at an insurance company. She and her coworkers experienced objects moving, as well as unexplainable noises. Carla's child may even have seen the ghost. "One night, I came in after hours to decorate for a coworker's birthday, and I had my six-year-old boy with me. He said, 'Mom, there is a man standing at the end of the hallway!' I looked, and there was no one there. I just shrugged it off as if it were no big deal so he wouldn't get scared. I hurried and got us the heck out of there!" said Carla.

So is there any truth to the legend of Old City Hall's haunting? I visited the Washington County Historical Society to find out. Only two city firemen were ever killed while on duty, Rudolph Schloemer and Edward F. Groth, but I found no reference to either being crushed at Old City Hall.

While the legend surrounding the building is probably just that, Vickie, Nick, and Carla are only a few of those who have experienced something unexplainable there. While the ghost of a firefighter probably isn't the culprit, that just makes their stories that much more intriguing to me. Who or what is the mysterious entity with the tender caress?

Section I: Northern Washington County

Image courtesy of Washington County Historical Society.

Directions

From Milwaukee: Take HWY 41/45 to West Bend. Exit at HWY 33, and head east.

From Fond du Lac: Take HWY 41 to Allenton. Exit at HWY 33, and head east.

From Madison: Take HWY 151 to Beaver Dam. Exit at HWY 33, and head east.

Once in West Bend: From HWY 33, turn south onto Seventh Avenue. Turn left onto Hickory Street. The building is to the left on the corner of Sixth and Hickory.

West Bend: Poplar Inn

The James Kneeland House is a beautiful two-and-a-half-story brick building. Built in 1858 by one of West Bend's founders, James Kneeland, the house is one of the oldest in the city. The little building has been a private residence, a Civil War–era inn, a beatnik coffeehouse, and even a paper company. Nowadays, it's occupied by the Poplar Inn.

Word around town is the inn offers a bit more than fine dining and a location convenient to West Bend's cultural district. It's also supposed to offer an encounter with a poltergeist.

According to former employees of the Poplar Inn, the Kneeland House poltergeist is a former owner's son who committed suicide in the attic.

Claims of the paranormal include entire kettles of soup being lifted off the stove and dumped on the floor by forces unknown and stemware hanging behind the bar being swept from their hooks by invisible hands; even the kitchen door has been vandalized by the entity. One night, during the dinner rush, the swinging door came down with a crash; the pins from its hinges were found lying neatly on the floor as if someone had simply taken them out.

The official word from the inn's management is that a previous owner's son did hang himself from a ceiling beam in the attic office above the bar. As for a haunting, they blame the poltergeist on overactive imaginations and the pops and creaks of a nearly 150-year-old building. Poltergeist or not, I do recommend that you visit the Poplar Inn. I'm not certain you'll see doors flying off hinges, but I'm sure you'll enjoy the food. My personal recommendation is the wild mushroom ravioli.

Section I: Northern Washington County

Image courtesy of Washington County Historical Society.

Directions

From Milwaukee: Take HWY 41/45 to West Bend. Exit at HWY 33, and head east.

From Fond du Lac: Take HWY 41 to Allenton. Exit at HWY 33, and head east.

From Madison: Take HWY 151 to Beaver Dam. Exit at HWY 33, and head east.

Once in West Bend: From HWY 33, turn south onto Seventh Avenue. Turn left onto Poplar Street. The restaurant is to the left on the corner of Poplar and Sixth.

West Bend: Rainbow Lake

It was an exceptionally hot August day as Joshua paddled sluggishly through the water. The mosquitos buzzing around his ears were enough to drive him mad. If only he had remembered to bring the bug spray.

His little rowboat sliced through the thick neon greens and yellows that mucked the surface of the small lake. Within moments, the algae and pollen swirled back together behind him, swallowing his wake.

The buzzing of the insects grew louder.

"All day and not a single fish," he grumbled to himself.

He swatted frantically at the ravenous mosquitos and gnats, and still, they would not let him be. Lifting his oar from the water, he sliced through the swarm, shouting obscenities. The oar slipped from his wet hands, flew through the air, and landed in the lake with a loud splash. Joshua's shoulders dropped as he sank back down into the boat.

He saw the oar floating beside a large piece of driftwood some twenty feet away. He reached his arm into the water and began paddling his way laboriously toward the oar. By the time he reached it, the thick, damp air clung to him even more, weighing him down. He reached out and took the oar, his boat coming to rest against a large log that bobbed in the water.

Using the oar, he tried to push against the log and send his boat in the direction of the shore. The log moved—far too easily, it seemed. It began to roll in the water alongside the boat. Joshua watched in amazement as one large eye looked at him. Its pupil narrowed, and a heavy, bark-colored eyelid slid closed over it. "The log" sank beneath the water, and

Joshua was once again alone on Rainbow Lake, though not for long. He didn't stay to see if the eye would return to the surface.

A Peculiar Theory

What you just read is based on an incident reported to me by a West Bend resident. It happened to a gentleman he knew from his own childhood, back when one could still fish in Rainbow Lake, which is now part of the Lac Lawrann Conservancy. For me, this story remains the most unusual and unique that I learned during my research. I spent many hours contemplating what he might have seen.

A possible answer came to me one day while I was reading John Boatman's book *Wisconsin American Indian History and Culture*. In his book, Boatman describes death and funerary customs for "many tribal groups in the Western Great Lakes region, including Wisconsin."

Several tribes believe that after life, the human soul will come to the Spirit River during its journey. The only path across the river is an enormous log. When the soul attempts to cross, the log begins to quake, as it is not a log after all, but a water sprit. The soul must then place *kinnickinnic* (tobacco) in the creature's hand so that it might cease its upheaval, allowing the soul to continue on its journey.

Did "Joshua" encounter a Native American water spirit? Wild speculation on my part, but as of now, I've no other explanation for a blinking log, unless, of course, the sighting occurred in Middle Earth, somewhere in or around Fangorn Forrest.

Bizarre Fact

In addition to Rainbow Lake, the Lac Lawrann Conservancy is home to a tiny graveyard along one of the property's hiking trails. Logs outline a rectangular patch of land parallel to the trail with numerous small stones acting as markers. A wooden sign engraved "Bird Cemetery 1955–1982" is the only source of information offered. Intrigued, I contacted the conservancy via their Facebook page to learn more. Here's the response:

"The Bird Cemetery was created by Lawrence and Ann Maurin, Lac Lawrann's founders. They were bird rehabilitators of sorts and helped hundreds of birds. Sixty did not survive and were buried there with their heads looking east, for the birds' calls were most beautiful in the rising sun. Each rock on the surface represents a bird that was buried."

There are no reports of phantom songbirds singing at sunrise, but just imagining that makes me happy.

Directions

From Milwaukee: Take HWY 41/45 to West Bend. Exit at HWY 33, and head east.

From Fond du Lac: Take HWY 41 to Allenton. Exit at HWY 33, and head east.

From Madison: Take HWY 151 to Beaver Dam. Exit at HWY 33, and head east.

Once in West Bend: From HWY 33, turn north onto Schmidt Road. Less than a mile ahead is the entrance driveway to Lac Lawrann Conservancy. Turn right into the driveway, and park in the lot. Grab a trail map and head to Rainbow Lake, located in the northeastern portion of the conservancy.

Section I: Northern Washington County

West Bend: Regner Park

Regner Park is considered the jewel of West Bend's park system. Originally envisioned by W. J. Wehle in the 1910s, Regner Park finally became a reality in 1930 when the park's namesake, West Bend Mayor Henry Regner, and the city council spent three thousand dollars to buy Goebel Woods.

As the years went by, more and more land was acquired, and now, Regner Park consists of ninety-one acres. There are double-tiered gazebos, sculptures, and even a garden labyrinth. A pleasanter park would be hard to find, but even this wonderful slice of Washington County is rumored to have its fair share of paranormal activity.

If I may borrow your imagination for a moment, picture yourself at twilight, walking across a small concrete footbridge. Silver Creek babbles underneath as you make your way past a little playground. Suddenly, you're surprised by the clear, joyful laughter of a little girl, though you didn't notice anyone as you approached.

Sure enough, you see a beautiful child there. Her father stands and watches with a smile on his face. He stoops down and calls to her, his arms open. She runs to him and gives him a huge, warm hug. But something just isn't right. You never heard a sound leave his lips. You can see the little girl is still laughing, but now, the only sound you can hear is the trill of chipping sparrows readying to roost.

The two figures become translucent and insubstantial. They disappear, as a cold chill snakes down your spine. While the thought of a family of two disappearing in front of the swings is unsettling, it's hardly nightmare fuel.

Regner's other ghost is a bit more worrisome. The malevolent apparition of a man with an umbrella is said to stalk the property. The very sight of him induces an overpowering sense of panic.

When I learned of these very different apparitions, I wondered if they might somehow be connected. Could this sinister figure be the reason the ghosts of the man and his daughter are trapped within the confines of the park? Was he a predator and they his prey? I did a bit of digging around and found that, according to West Bend residents, people have died at Regner. One man suffered a fatal injury while diving in one of the ponds. On another occasion, a woman was discovered dead in her car, but no foul play was suspected. Neither incident seems to mesh with any of the known apparitions. If something ghastly did happen there, it remains undiscovered.

The wooded areas of Regner Park have their own peculiar legend. By day, the well-maintained wooded trails are idyllic. Were it not for the sound of nearby traffic, one could easily forget that he or she is still inside an urban center. Yet it's said that when the sun sets, the woods are—and please pardon this groan-inducing cliché—as different as night is to day.

Sightings of shadow beings are not uncommon in the woods at night. For those unfamiliar with these creatures, shadow beings are black forms that resemble people but are usually associated with nonhuman hauntings. That is to say, they are often considered to be demonic in nature. The woods themselves are said to become menacing and mischievous, tormenting those brave enough to travel them after nightfall.

When I first moved to West Bend in 2007, I wasn't aware of Regner's legends. I would often walk there and sit beside Silver Creek with my MP3 player, contemplating what the future held for me in my new home. I never saw the father and daughter ghosts, or if I did, I never recognized them for what they were. I didn't encounter the umbrella-toting specter, nor did I spend any time in the woods surrounding the park past dark. So is there any truth to all this? There is only one way to find out, I decided: go to Regner at night, and see what happens.

It was a warm summer afternoon when I made my decision. A light rain was falling. By the time night came, the rain had gone and stars were dotting the sky. I felt that, with the stars out, I should be plenty brave enough to deal with any shadow person or mischievous tree. But just in case, I badgered my wife until she agreed to go with me. I lessened the blow to my ego a bit by rationalizing that it isn't safe to legend-trip alone.

Section I: Northern Washington County

I can prove that this is true by pointing out I previously said so in this book's introduction.

We arrived at Regner's empty parking lot just past 9:00 p.m. and headed to the woods, flashlights and bug spray in hand. At the haunted playground, there was neither sight nor sound of a father and daughter, otherworldly or otherwise. Luckily, there was no menace with an umbrella either.

After a while, we continued toward the swimming pond, until we saw a heavily wooded path to our left. *Now or never,* I thought, and in we went. I immediately got creeped out upon entering the woods. The light from our flashlights bounced all over, casting shadows in every direction. *It would be hard to spot a shadow person at all,* I thought. The raindrops were still dripping down from where they had been caught in the canopy, making it sound as if there was movement all around us. A couple of times, I swear I heard whispers. It is also worth noting how distant streetlights partially obscured by trees can closely resemble a pair of peering eyes.

Even after we acclimated to our eerie surroundings, I still felt very uncomfortable and nervous. There are so many places someone or something can hide in the woods, especially at night, not to mention that it was impossible to hear anything approaching. My wife turned to me. "Well, I don't really feel anything out here—" she began, only to interrupt herself with a shout of "Oh my God!" I whirled to look where she was facing. My flashlight lit up, and most definitely blinded, three teenage girls.

"Sorry," one said flatly, rather unimpressed by our cowardice.

"Just trying to get home," said another. They likely made fun of us as soon as they got out of earshot, though who could blame them?

We waited a while longer. I continued to hear footsteps and whispers, but given the conditions, how could I make the claim that it was something paranormal? Frustrated and fearful of further disgracing myself in front of another group of park patrons, I decided we should call it quits.

A month later, I revisited Regner at night, this time with fellow members of the Paranormal Investigation and Research Society (PIRS) and a contingent from the Wisconsin Area Paranormal Society (WAPS). We found no apparitions or shadow people, and the trees let us be. A couple of drainage ditches nearly claimed our lives, but that was all. Of course, it doesn't mean the legends aren't valid. After all, if paranormal activity occurred on command, it would just be called normal activity, wouldn't it? Legends aside, Regner Park is a wonderful place, and I encourage readers to take advantage of everything it has to offer, paranormal or otherwise.

Bizarre Fact

Regner Park turned one hundred years old in 2010. To celebrate, the City of West Bend and a committee called Celebrate Regner sponsored an attempt to hold the world's largest "Thriller" dance. On July 31, 1,935 Wisconsinites gathered, many dressed as zombies, Michael Jackson, or a combination of both, to earn Wisconsin the United States record! Noteworthy dancers included the Milwaukee Wave Professional Dance Team, the Milwaukee Brewers Diamond Dancers, and the Klements Racing Sausages. Sadly, Mexico still holds the *Guinness Book* world record with more than thirteen thousand dancers. Still, score one for Washington County!

Directions

From Milwaukee: Take HWY 41/45 to West Bend. Exit at HWY 33, and head east.

From Fond du Lac: Take HWY 41 to Allenton. Exit at HWY 33, and head east.

From Madison: Take HWY 151 to Beaver Dam. Exit at HWY 33, and head east.

Once in West Bend: From HWY 33, turn north onto Seventh Avenue/North Main Street. Less than a mile ahead is the entrance to Regner Park. Turn left into the driveway. Turn left from the driveway, and go to the far end of the parking lot. The playground is on the other side of Silver Creek.

Section I: Northern Washington County

West Bend: Restat Building

Since its construction in 1897, the former Restat Building has been many things: a high school, the city library, and even a recreation center. The building's role within the community is constantly changing. The only thing that has endured at the beautiful old building is Janitor Jim.

Image courtesy of Washington County Historical Society.

The stories about the building's long-standing phantasm go back as far as anyone can remember. As is often the case with legends, the details regarding Janitor Jim's demise vary. Some versions of the tale say he hanged himself in the basement; others say it was in the attic.

Folks who have worked in the building say doors slam on their own, cold spots abound, and footsteps echo down empty corridors.

Jackie Maynard worked there when it was occupied by the Recreation and Forestry Department. The following quote was found in speaker's notes from the Washington County Historical Society's Halloween event "Ghosts of Washington County."

"Jim seems to be friendly, but he does move items around. He tends to mess with females and usually shows up after 10:00 p.m.," said Jackie.

The goriest Janitor Jim legend involves his repeated manifestation in an attic window. The window will illuminate a stark scarlet, followed by the appearance of Jim, dangling by his neck.

Armed with this information, I took a nighttime stroll past the building. I discovered that when you reach the corner of Eighth Avenue and Elm Street, while walking north, there really is a red glow in the uppermost window. My heart skipped a beat until I realized that it was an exit sign. That could explain the scarlet light, but it doesn't explain reports of seeing the apparition of a hanged man.

Representatives from Restat, LLC, a prescription benefit management firm that most recently occupied the building, said that as of 2006, no Janitor Jim shenanigans had occurred. Of course, Restat has since relocated to Milwaukee. According to a 2009 *West Bend Daily News* article, the official word from Restat was that they needed more space and that Milwaukee was closer to their home office. Did Jim turn them into believers one night by appearing with a noose around his neck, his eyes bulging, basked in a crimson glow? I spoke with a lady who worked at Restat when it was in West Bend, and she said Jim was still very much a presence there. If I'm allowed some bad gallow's humor, it seems Jim is still hanging around.

Directions

From Milwaukee: Take HWY 41/45 to West Bend. Exit at HWY 33, and head east.

From Fond du Lac: Take HWY 41 to Allenton. Exit at HWY 33, and head east.

From Madison: Take HWY 151 to Beaver Dam. Exit at HWY 33, and head east.

Section I: Northern Washington County

Once in West Bend: From HWY 33, turn south onto Seventh Avenue. Turn right onto Elm Street. The building is to the right on the corner of Eighth and Elm.

West Bend: Silver Creek Apartments

The Silver Creek Apartments Complex, located at the intersection of Highway 33 and Highway 45, looks about as ordinary as an apartment complex can look, but does it have a dark past? Former residents of Silver Creek Apartments claim the original complex owner, who had "issues dealing with stress," allegedly hanged himself from the roof of the building and haunts the rooftop.

According to notes from the Washington County Historical Society's 2005 "Ghosts of Washington County" program, tenants claim to hear him pacing back and forth, as if contemplating his own demise. Individuals have also reported seeing his apparition on the rooftop during full moons, and sightings seem to happen more frequently near Halloween.

I've been unable to learn much about the building and can neither confirm nor deny whether a former landlord killed himself on the property. Drive by during an autumn full moon to investigate, but please don't trespass. If you want to know if you can hear him from a second-floor apartment, I recommend you sign a lease.

Directions

From Milwaukee: Take HWY 41/45 to West Bend. Exit at HWY 33, and head east.

From Fond du Lac: Take HWY 41 to Allenton. Exit at HWY 33, and head east.

Section I: Northern Washington County

From Madison: Take HWY 151 to Beaver Dam. Exit at HWY 33, and head east.

Once in West Bend: The apartment building is on the north side of HWY 33.

West Bend: University of Wisconsin-Washington County and Ridge Run County Park

Carl Pick was one of the most accomplished men in Washington County during his lifetime. Born in 1888, he became a successful businessman in the fields of manufacturing, publishing, brewing, and farming. By the 1940s, Carl had acquired 187-acres of land outside the city of West Bend. This property, called the Pick Farm, was Carl's sanctuary. When he needed a break from his various industries, Carl would roam around the lakes and ponds of the farm duck hunting, usually accompanied by a pack of pups.

In early 1959, Carl suffered a bad fall in his home. He went on with life as usual, noticing no apparent injury. It wouldn't be long after the fall, however, that Carl slipped into a coma. He was taken to old St. Joseph's hospital in West Bend where he was diagnosed with a fractured skull, only to pass away a short time later. Carl's body was interred at Pick Farm at a secluded section of the property alongside the graves of many of his most beloved dogs.

It was Carl's dream that he would one day see his farm become a park, so that everyone might enjoy the land as much as he and his family had. According to a quote from his son Bob, found in the *Carl S. Pick Memorial Ceremony of Dedication* pamphlet, "[H]e was a down-to-earth man who was just interested in doing what was right for West Bend."

In the early 1960s, West Bend was selected as a potential home for a new University of Wisconsin extension. It was decided the Pick Farm would be an ideal location for the new school. The city bought the property. Eighty-seven acres were set aside for what would become the University of Wisconsin-Washington County (UW-WC), while the remainder became a county park called Ridge Run, named thusly for a glacial esker that winds through the narrow park.

Image courtesy of Washington County Historical Society.

A couple of years following the opening of the school and park, Carl Pick's remains were disinterred from his original grave near the University Drive entrance of Ridge Run and reinterred at Washington County Memorial Park. Not long after that, rumors of paranormal activity began to surface, especially concerning the new university.

I first became aware of the supposed UW-WC haunting at the Washington County Historical Society's 2008 "Ghosts of Washington County" program. The storyteller on stage spoke of a custodian at the school who'd regularly heard strange noises, found classrooms in shambles from an unknown and apparently unexplainable source, and even witnessed light switches being flipped on and off by unseen hands. The story climaxed with several custodians being chased out of the school one night by the crashing of tables and chairs as the apparent poltergeist put an exclamation point on the announcement of its existence.

This haunting is very intriguing to me. Many paranormal phenomena are rather subtle—a shadowy figure seen from the corner of your eye, the sound of unexplained footsteps, perhaps a phantom moan in the darkness—but this is a blatant, over-the-top, destructive force. Would Carl Pick, a man who always wanted the best for West Bend, really cause such chaos at its only university?

I went to the Washington County Historical Society to find answers. There, I found a book about Carl called *Let Me Tell You One Thing!*, which was compiled by family and friends. The book contains poems and lyrics composed by Carl, as well as many personal memories of him. I found the anecdotes from his widow Maybelle "Mibs" Pick-Hill particularly interesting and entertaining. The first revolves around Carl's trip to Nazi Germany for the infamous 1936 Olympics in Berlin. Carl was once president of the Wisconsin State Bowling Associating and was accompanying the US Olympic bowling team. Mibs states that while there, he purchased a cuckoo clock, which he had shipped back to West Bend. Mibs concluded that the clock "cuckooed every fifteen minutes. Finally, Carl got sick of that cuckoo, so he shot it."

Mibs next anecdote involved Carl's ongoing rivalry with the sparrows who frequented his sleeping porch. Each morning, they'd perch on the thick vines clinging to the porch and wake Carl with their song. Each time, he'd run at the birds, swinging with his fishing pole to scare them away. Despite his continual efforts, the sparrows would always return a half hour later.

The other stories painted a picture of a man who loved his family and the outdoors. While these stories from Mibs do indicate Carl had a slightly eccentric temper, I still couldn't understand why he'd be the cause of the university's haunting. Could the fact he'd been exhumed cause all this? If so, why was he ransacking the school? He wasn't even buried on UW-WC property.

While I ruminated on the UW-WC haunting, I was contacted by Alan Gee. Alan is a founding member of the Wisconsin Area Paranormal Society (WAPS) a paranormal investigation group located in East Central Wisconsin that originally formed in West Bend in 1988.

From Alan, I learned about several rumored hauntings in the county, but what caught my eye on his e-mailed list of hauntings was Ridge Run. I assumed he meant the UW-WC haunting. When I spoke with him about it, he said that the Ridge Run legend didn't have anything to do with Carl Pick or his exhumation. According to Alan, a young man is rumored to have killed himself in the woods near the Scenic Drive park entrance in the 1960s. Certain visitors have reported seeing his apparition wandering toward the woods only to vanish shortly before reaching the

Section I: Northern Washington County

tree line. Someone who commits suicide is more likely to be the source of a negative, violent haunting than a man like Carl Pick.

Since I learned of the legend of the hanged man, I've been trying to validate the story. As of yet, I've only uncovered the story of a young girl who was fatally injured while sledding in 2002. Meanwhile, officials at UW-WC responded to my inquiries regarding their haunting with curt, one-sentence replies denying ever having heard of any paranormal activity from students or faculty.

For now, the reason for the school's and park's respective hauntings remains a mystery. One thing is certain: Carl Pick remains well known in his beloved hometown—not only because of his accomplishments in life, but also because of his alleged activities in the afterlife.

Directions

For Ridge Run County Park:

From Milwaukee: Take HWY 41/45 to West Bend. Exit at HWY 33, and head east.

From Fond du Lac: Take HWY 41 to Allenton. Exit at HWY 33, and head east.

From Madison: Take HWY 151 to Beaver Dam. Exit at HWY 33, and head east.

Once in West Bend: From HWY 33, turn south onto University Drive. Less than half a mile ahead is the entrance to Ridge Run County Park. Turn right into the driveway. Follow the road down the hill. The abandoned cemetery was located in this area. Turn right, and drive through the parking lot. Follow the road from the turnabout to the other side of the park where the ghost has been spotted.

For UW-WC:

From Milwaukee: Take HWY 41/45 to West Bend. Exit at HWY 33, and head east.

From Fond du Lac: Take HWY 41 to Allenton. Exit at HWY 33, and head east.

From Madison: Take HWY 151 to Beaver Dam. Exit at HWY 33, and head east.

Once in West Bend: From HWY 33, turn south onto University Drive. Less than half a mile ahead is the entrance driveway to the University of Wisconsin-Washington County.

Section I: Northern Washington County

West Bend: Wallace Lake

Certain residents around Wallace Lake have experienced a peculiar phenomenon for years: the sound of phantom drums, as steady as a heartbeat, ancient and sad. The lake itself is a fifty-two-acre body of water located just outside of West Bend that, oddly enough, is shaped like a Native American arrowhead, though admittedly, one crudely made.

Charlie Hintz, owner of an alternative-art website called WisconsinSickness.com, grew up on the shores of Wallace Lake. He recalls one occasion when something besides a bluegill was hauled out of the water, and it just might hold a clue to the mystery of the phantom drums.

"Some people from my neighborhood were scuba diving, and they found a skeleton in the muck on the bottom of the lake. Its skull was covered by debris, some kind of cloth or bucket.

"They grabbed a shinbone to prove they really saw it, then called the police. The general consensus was that it was a shunned Native American. No one was ever able to relocate the rest of the remains. The shinbone was similar in size to a four-year-old child's."

During my investigation, I couldn't find any official record regarding the incident or the whereabouts of the mysterious shinbone, so I decided to research the burial customs of Wisconsin's native peoples. After studying numerous detailed descriptions of Native American funerary practices, I didn't find any reference to water burial, much less specific practices for disposing of a "shunned" tribe member.

If the story regarding the found skeleton is genuine and not merely neighborhood folklore, it seems much more likely to me that the child drowned and couldn't be inhumed by his or her people. Maybe the phantom drums of Wallace Lake are music from a time long gone and those still mourning the loss of a child taken too soon from the physical world.

Directions

From Milwaukee: Take HWY 41/45 to West Bend. Exit at HWY 33, and head east.

From Fond du Lac: Take HWY 41 to Allenton. Exit at HWY 33, and head east.

From Madison: Take HWY 151 to Beaver Dam. Exit at HWY 33, and head east.

Once in West Bend: From HWY 33, turn north onto HWY 144 N/N Main St. Follow HWY 144 out of West Bend. Turn a slight right onto Wallace Lake Road at the large curve in the road. Turn left onto River Road. Go about a quarter mile. The public access/boat launch is on the left side.

Section I: Northern Washington County

West Bend: Washington County Memorial Park

Washington County Memorial Park is a fifty-five-acre cemetery at the intersection of Paradise Drive and Eighteenth Avenue. The cemetery has a reputation for being haunted, though only a little. Reports are limited to two very classic phenomena: cold spots and spook lights.

I visited the cemetery on a warm summer afternoon, since a cold patch of air would be hard to explain away. While there, I experienced nothing strange unless one considers the cemetery's colony of gargantuan squirrels to be paranormal. Since they weren't quite large enough to make off with my entire body, such a proclamation would be hyperbole.

Later that night, I decided to drive by the cemetery hoping to see some spook lights or, perhaps if I were lucky, a glowing apparition. When I arrived at the adjacent intersection, I was incredibly confused as to what I was looking at. What had been a cemetery in daylight now appeared to be lit like a city skyline in miniature. But these lights were not supernatural, only solar. Nearly all the graves in the cemetery are decorated with small, ornamental solar lights making it impossible to determine a spook light from a garden light.

My research was unable to determine how long ago the first rumors of ghost lights in Memorial Park surfaced. If they'd been circulating since the 1930s when the cemetery was first established, the sightings couldn't be explained away as twenty-first-century mourning technology. But that's an "if." Just when I was ready to write this one off, I was contacted by a young lady who wishes to remain anonymous.

In October 2011, my husband, my fourteen-year-old son, and I were driving east into West Bend on Paradise Road. Just as we were nearing town, I saw three amber lights above and between the treetops. I pulled over and told everyone to look. The huge amber balls of light were in a field, and they were so low and large, we couldn't believe it. They slowly moved in front of one another, making no sound.

Several cars passed by us as this was happening, and one even stopped to watch. About a minute passed, then I tried to video-record it with my phone, but the device's memory was full. As I watched the lights through the screen, they disappeared one by one.

Since this happened, I've been searching for anyone else who saw the lights. From West Bend, the lights may have looked as if they were over the cemetery and not in the field.

Have the spook lights people have reportedly seen in Memorial Park actually been hovering over nearby fields? And if so, what are they? This sighting reminds me of an unexplainable amber orb of light I witnessed in West Bend on a summer night in 2007. I saw a similar globe of light in the northern sky while walking down Fifth Avenue just past dusk. It didn't move or make a sound, and after several minutes, it faded away, as if on a dimmer, and never returned.

It resembled a streetlight, but it was too high in the sky to be one, as it appeared to be higher up than the Old Courthouse Museum tower, the second highest point in the entire county. While this doesn't prove there are spook lights in Memorial Park, it does illustrate that people are seeing strange lights nearby. Are these balls of light supernatural, perhaps even extraterrestrial, in origin? The next time you're in West Bend at night, keep your eyes pointed at the sky—unless you're driving of course.

DIRECTIONS

From Milwaukee: Take HWY 41/45 to West Bend. Exit at Paradise Road, and head west.

From Fond du Lac: Take HWY 41 to Allenton. Exit at HWY 33, and head east to HWY 45. Take HWY 45 south to Paradise Road. Exit at Paradise Road, and head west.

From Madison: Take HWY 151 to Beaver Dam. Exit at HWY 33, and head east to HWY 45. Take HWY 45 south to Paradise Road. Exit at Paradise Road, and head west.

Once in West Bend: From Paradise Road, turn north onto Eighteenth Avenue. The driveway entrance is about a tenth of a mile on the left. Follow the main road. At the fork, follow the road right. Turn right at the next crossroad. The Pick marker is on the left (see University of Wisconsin-Washington County and Ridge Run County Park).

West Bend: Washington House

When I first began researching this book, one location kept coming up over and over again in conversation—the Washington House. Whenever I'd talk about the book I was working on or inquire about haunted places within the county, at least one person would mention the nearly 150-year-old building in downtown West Bend.

"Have you heard about the Washington House?" someone would say.

"The old hotel? What about it?" I'd usually reply.

"Is it haunted?"

"I've not heard anything. Why? Is it supposed to be?"

"Oh, it must be!"

The Washington House was once one of the most marvelous buildings in West Bend. Over the years, many prominent Americans have visited it. Former US presidents John F. Kennedy and Ronald W. Reagan have slept and dined there respectively. These days, however, after decades of thoughtless remodeling, neglect, and harsh Wisconsin winters, it looks like any other tired old building you might have seen before. In its youth, it was a fine, thriving hotel with a wine cellar renowned as far away as St. Louis. These days, the upper floors are used as apartments while the lower floor holds a pub.

One cold November night, while walking through downtown, a friend and I passed by the Washington House. She was familiar with my research and knew how many inquiries I'd gotten regarding the place. Instead of the standard, "Is it haunted?" she said something unexpected: "So who do you think haunts the Washington House?"

I didn't hesitate. "If anyone haunts it, Balthasar Goetter would."

She chuckled and replied, "Who is Balthasar Goetter, and why him?"

Section I: Northern Washington County

"He built the hotel, twice. And furthermore, if you're named Balthasar, you're practically destined to leave an impression on everything around you."

Though I was born about a hundred years too late to know anything about Balthasar firsthand, my assumption about him is based on more than his formidable given name.

Image courtesy of Washington County Historical Society.

Balthasar was born in 1817 in German Hesse-Darmstadt and emigrated from there to the United States in 1846. He had learned the brewing trade in Europe, so he quickly found employment at Levi Blossom's brewery in Milwaukee, where he worked for two years.

In 1849, Bathasar visited the small settlement of West Bend, which at that time consisted of roughly a dozen families, with the hopes of starting his own brewery.

Dorothy E. Williams's book, *The Spirit of West Bend* chronicles Bathasar's early days in West Bend. When he got to the newborn community, Bathasar thought it a fine location for a business because of the constant flow of traffic passing through from Milwaukee to Fond du Lac, though he feared he'd be lonely. Two friends of his by the name of Mayers knew just the cure for loneliness: a bride. His friends had a sister back home they thought would be perfect for him. The problem was "back home" meant back in Germany.

The tenacious Balthasar wasn't daunted. He left straightaway for the old country. He made the six-week trip to Germany, got engaged, and then brought her back with him. He built the West Bend Brewing Company, which doubled as their home, out of logs. A more appropriate beer-foam romance novel could hardly be imagined and seems particularly fitting, considering Wisconsin's love affair with hops and barley. Unfortunately, Balthazar contracted a terrible eye infection, forcing him to retire from the brewery and leave it to his brothers-in-law.

While his life as a beer baron wasn't meant to be, it would take much more than that to stop a man who'd traveled from Germany to America, back to Germany, and then back to America, all in the hopes of making something of himself.

In 1852, Bathasar opened the first Washington House, which was a wooden-frame hotel. The hotel did extremely well for twelve years, until on New Year's Day, 1864, it burned to the ground. Only a cast-iron stove remained, and it was blamed for the blaze.

Most of us would be devastated to see our home and business reduced to a heap of ash. Most likely, so was Balthasar, though he left himself little time for self-pity. He began rebuilding at once and put up a new Washington House atop the remains of the old. By October of the same year, a bigger, better three-story brick hotel was open.

An 1865 advertisement described it as "a commodious three-story brick hotel on the site of the old Washington House." It touted "a good stable with attractive hostlers and well supplied with hay and grain."

For more than twenty more years, Goetter ran the second Washington House until misfortune again crashed into his life. In 1887, his son John, who was an incredibly successful businessman himself, died unexpectedly. This was a far greater blow to Bathasar than any illness or fire. Bathasar and his wife sold the hotel and retired the next year.

In 1889, Bathasar traveled Washington Territory in the Pacific Northwest to visit some of his children. On his way back to Wisconsin, he took sick in California with an inflammation of the lungs. He barely made it back to his daughter's home in Milwaukee, where he passed away quietly at the age of seventy-two.

After relating much of this information to my friend—in far less detail, of course—I realized we were nearly to my front door.

"So Balthasar's the ghost of the Washington House, huh?" she asked.

Section I: Northern Washington County

Image courtesy of Washington County Historical Society.

"He could be, but it could be anyone. That building was a hotel for much of its existence. Lots of people stay at hotels. Lots of people die at hotels too. I've heard rumors it was used for bootlegging during prohibition, though I've not found any evidence to support that. I have no idea if it's even haunted. I'm just guessing, wishing actually."

"Wishing?"

"Yeah, wouldn't that be a great ending to Bathasar's story? '...and his ghost still resides at the Washington House to this day!' That's a far better ending to Bathasar's story. If anyone had the gumption to hang around after death, I think he did."

My friend smiled at me, likely thinking me the biggest dork in all of southeastern Wisconsin.

"Get inside. Go to sleep. G'night," she said.

After all my research, after months of inquiries within the community, I'd found zero reports of paranormal activity at the old place. Then a young woman by the name of Christine contacted me about an experience she'd had while renting an apartment at the Washington House.

One afternoon, she was reading when she spied movement from the corner of her eye. She turned and watched as a stick of deodorant smoothly slid two feet across a table and fell on the ground "like it was being pushed."

Perhaps the place is haunted—if not by ghosts, definitely by history. Whether or not Bathasar is still there, we'll likely never know.

Directions

From Milwaukee: Take HWY 41/45 to West Bend. Exit at HWY 33, and head east.

From Fond du Lac: Take HWY 41 to Allenton. Exit at HWY 33, and head east.

From Madison: Take HWY 151 to Beaver Dam. Exit at HWY 33, and head east.

Once in West Bend: From HWY 33, turn south onto Seventh Avenue. Turn left onto Elm Street. Turn left onto Sixth Avenue, which ends at Main Street. The building is to the left on the corner of Sixth and Main.

Section I: Northern Washington County

West Bend: West Bend Theatre

And through all the years of my existence, I will continue to bid you welcome in unfailing friendliness...it thrills me to see your faces...[sic] but what will thrill me most is when all West Bend will say—THE WEST BEND THEATRE IS THE FINEST THEATRE FOR US IN ALL THE WORLD. —The Voice of the Theatre, from a West Bend Theatre program, circa 1930

A brilliant old sign hangs in downtown West Bend spelling out the city's name in warm, incandescent light. While there are more than a few pubs in the vicinity, the sign isn't there to remind beery revelers of their present whereabouts. It marks the location of the West Bend Theatre. When it was constructed in 1929, the theatre was the city's amusement mecca. But in 2009, the two-screen theatre folded, unable to compete with modern multiplexes. Since then, it has sat quiet, but not empty, if the legends are true.

The haunting supposedly began the night of the building's last play, hours before motion pictures would permanently replace the theatre's dedicated troupe of thespians. The play's leading man was particularly distraught after his final performance and hanged himself from the second-floor balcony.

Twenty-something-year-old April Shaw grew up in West Bend and had this to share. "The theatre on the second floor had problems with the film reels mysteriously catching on fire. One of my younger sisters had her money refunded a number of occasions. Once, in 1995, the film reel suddenly burst into flames as she tried to watch *Casper*." Perhaps a movie about a friendly ghost was too much for the disgruntled stage actor to take?

Other stories I heard involved a shadowy figure vanishing into the movie screen and dusty footprints that appeared to walk through film vault doors, which had rusted shut with age.

Image courtesy of Washington County Historical Society.

I went down to the Washington County Historical Society to see if I could find any information on the theatre's tragic leading man, and it turns out the legend is just a legend. The West Bend Theatre was never a performing-arts theatre. From the day it opened on November 26, 1929, it was a movie house. Though it did present vaudeville shows on the weekends, I found no reference to suicides there by any local Abbotts and/or Costellos. Though the legend of the suicidal leading man was debunked, it didn't mean the place wasn't haunted. I was determined to find a former theatre employee who might provide some insight into its paranormal activity. After months with no luck, I'd all but given up when Lester Hahn overheard me talking about my quest in a downtown West Bend restaurant.

According to Lester, he and other employees of the theatre used to credit the haunting to a former manager by the name of Roland "Rollie" Mead, who passed away on the theater's stairs from a heart attack in the early 1990s. Rollie was known for wearing a large set of keys on his hip. Numerous times, theatre projectionists would hear footsteps outside the projection booth, accompanied by Rollie's signature "jingle." When they'd open the door, no one would be there. Lester also recalled once when he encountered what he thought might be Rollie while sitting in the theatre's office with a manager. The two men were having a conversation when they both heard the familiar sound of Rollie's keys. They turned and watched as the doorknob began to turn. Initially thinking someone was having trouble entering the office, Lester opened the door to find the hallway empty.

Lester gave no hint that he or other employees were ever scared of the ghost. He seemed to remember Mr. Mead rather fondly even though Rollie fired him. Twice.

I dearly hope the West Bend Theatre reopens. I'll be first in line for a midnight showing regardless of who is haunting it. It would thrill me greatly to hear the voice of the West Bend Theatre in person—and maybe see a ghost or two if that's not asking too much.

Directions

From Milwaukee: Take HWY 41/45 to West Bend. Exit at HWY 33, and head east.

From Fond du Lac: Take HWY 41 to Allenton. Exit at HWY 33, and head east.

From Madison: Take HWY 151 to Beaver Dam. Exit at HWY 33, and head east.

Once in West Bend: From HWY 33, turn south onto Seventh Avenue. Turn left onto Hickory Street. Turn left onto Main Street. The theater is on the right.

Section II: Central Washington County

Hartford: Kettle Moraine Road

Pike Lake State Park is nestled between the City of Hartford and the Village of Slinger in the middle of the Kettle Moraine State Forest. The forest runs from Southern Wisconsin all the way to Lake Winnebago. This particular park is named after the 522-acre glacial lake located inside it.

Pike Lake is an enormous spring-fed kettle.

Here's the layperson's explanation of a kettle from someone rather experienced at being a layperson. Kettles are large depressions made by glacial ice that broke away from icebergs during the last ice age. This ice was covered by gravel and silt from the glaciers as they receded. Eventually, the ice under this debris melted, causing everything above it to sink down. In this example, the depression slowly filled with spring water, creating Pike Lake. By contrast, moraines are mounds of glacial debris that didn't have a pocket of ice beneath to cause a depression and instead left behind a hilly land formation.

To access Pike Lake State Park and all its ice age wonders, turn south off State Highway 60 onto very hilly and curvy Kettle Moraine Road. Just as you leave the highway, you'll start up a large hill—a hill that has allegedly claimed at least one life.

Legends and hauntings involving car accidents are plentiful in America, and there's no wonder. Close to forty thousand people die in fatal car accidents each year in the United States. It's a wonder the highways and back roads of this country aren't gridlocked coast to coast with ectoplasmic accident victims.

The fateful haunt-inducing accident on Kettle Moraine Road allegedly took place sometime during the 1970s. A young man was driving far too fast coming down that large hill, lost control, and was killed when his car careened into the trees. Since then, his presence has persisted on that hill he failed to respect. You'll sometimes encounter his ghost, covered in blood, trying to flag down someone to help him. Motorists who have been decent enough to stop to try to help the young man get out of their car only to find themselves standing alone on a hill in the woods, left to wonder what just happened.

I was unable to find evidence that someone died on that hill in a car accident in the 1970s, but given the alarming data on fatal car accidents, it's likely someone did. If you go in search of this legend, do drive carefully.

Directions

From Milwaukee and Fond du Lac: Take HWY 41 to Slinger. Exit at HWY 60, and head west.

From Madison: Take HWY 151 north to Columbus. Exit at HWY 60, and follow it east.

Once in Hartford: From HWY 60, turn south onto Kettle Moraine Road, which leads into Pike Lake State Park.

Hartford: Schauer Arts and Activities Center

What's the first thing you think of when you read the words "canned foods"? Fallout shelters or high sodium levels, perhaps? Whatever it is, I bet it isn't ghosts. But according to the kindly folks at the Schauer Arts and Activities Center, this former cannery-turned-bastion-of-the-arts has preserved a lot more than corned beef and pumpkin. Three different entities are said to roam the building, each having supposedly died tragically on the premises. These are the origins of the Schauer's unnerving trifecta of entities, as related to Schauer staff by various members of the Hartford community.

A Little Girl Wandering Alone

Most parents know the frustrations of being unable to find a sitter for their child, especially in an era when both parents normally work. These days, when there's no one to look after your child, you have to call in and risk the consequences. However, there once was a time when parents simply brought their child to work if in such a pinch, even if they worked in the hazardous environment of a cannery.

The Schauer's most tragic purported ghost is a little girl. One day, her father was forced to bring his daughter to work. The girl strayed from her inattentive parent, wandered into the loading area of the cannery, and walked behind one of the trucks. The driver, unable to see her small frame, backed over her, killing her instantly. Since that terrible day, the apparition of the little girl has been frequently sighted near the old loading docks, which is now the Schauer's second floor.

Technical Director Randy Schultz saw a girl playing unattended during a phase of the building's remodeling, shortly after the Schauer opened. He watched as she ran into a then-unfinished portion of the building's second floor, which is now a kitchen area. Fearing for the girl's safety, he followed her. When he got to there, he found himself alone. There was no way she could have left the construction area without passing by him.

Image courtesy of Washington County Historical Society.

The Scandalous Screamer

The Schauer's second legend is a bit more sordid. I doubt anyone reading this can say they've never found a coworker sexually attractive. While most never take such attractions beyond the realm of flirtation, a young woman from the cannery's front office did, and she's apparently still paying for her poor judgment to this day.

Not long after the woman began an office love affair, her lifeless body was discovered slumped over her own desk early one morning. Allegations of foul play were whispered, but nothing ever became of them. The legend is painfully lacking in detail—especially regarding how long the affair lasted or how, or even if, she was killed. There's also no word on if the motivation was jealousy or secrecy.

Her high heels have been heard throughout the Schauer. One Schauer employee I spoke with even heard her voice in a second-floor hallway. "I heard a woman call out to me; it sounded like she said, 'Hey come here!' I thought it was a nearby coworker, but it wasn't; after that, we both hightailed it out of there."

Her ghostly screams occasionally echo through the building. "You can't make out any words or anything, but she sounds like she's calling for help."

Turn Out the Lights!

The third entity is nicknamed "Ralph." He's the troublemaker of the group. This former machine operator supposedly died while on the job at the cannery. Some stories say a heart attack did him in; other versions insist it was a stroke. Regardless of the cause, Ralph has apparently refused to move on from the cannery, and he still has a fascination with technology. While his apparition is occasionally seen in the second-floor theater seats, dressed in overalls, his deeds are much more infamous than his brief appearances.

Ralph is often blamed for putting equipment where it shouldn't be. He's also fond of playing with the lights. One night, following a performance, a Schauer employee could not get the lights in the theater to turn off, no matter what she did. She pressed every combination of buttons possible and flipped every switch. Finally out of frustration, she called out, "Ralph, I'm not leaving until these lights are off!" A second later, the theater went dark. She decided it best to keep her word and promptly left.

"It seems most of the activity is late at night. Most of the time, Ralph and the others are pretty well behaved, but when you work late, the energy changes. It's like the ghosts get anxious because you're not supposed to be there," said a Schauer employee.

The Investigation

I attempted to find out if any of the three deaths at the cannery really occurred, but I was unsuccessful. I did talk with one gentleman who had a friend who worked at the cannery in the 1940s, around the time of the three rumored deaths. His friend was accidentally doused with boiling water. He saved himself from a death by scalding by jumping into a vat of cold water. Certainly, the cannery was a dangerous place.

Having failed to verify the historical aspects of the building's ghosts, I wanted to see if the Paranormal Investigation and Research Society (PIRS) could capture any evidence of the reported haunting, and the folks at the Schauer were eager to oblige.

After a late-night tour with Randy Schultz, the gentleman who saw the apparition of the little girl, we were left on our own. While the Schauer's

Section II: Central Washington County

spirits have never harmed anyone, Randy wasn't eager to encounter any more ghosts.

The night was uneventful as we sought Ralph and the high-heeled lady. It wasn't until we began searching for the little girl that activity started to pick up.

I was standing alone on the stage waiting on the other PIRS-ers to return from an electronic voice phenomena (EVP) recording session, when, from the corner of my eye, I saw the distinct shape of a head and shoulders, child-sized and feminine, duck, ironically, behind the stage's ghost light. I hurried over but found nothing unusual.

It should be told that in theater-speak, a "ghost light" is a lamp with a naked bulb that's left lit all night. Often, it's left on for safety's sake, to prevent anyone from walking off a dark stage and injuring themselves. However, the theater world is a superstitious one, and these lamps also have supernatural significance. One superstition is that a light left lit onstage at night allows the spirits of dead thespians to continue to perform, so they won't plague the productions of the living. The other ghost light superstition is completely contrary, saying it can hold ghosts at bay. If this latter superstition is the purpose of the ghost light at the Schauer, it doesn't seem to be working.

Not long after my possible ghost sighting, the others returned from upstairs near the art gallery. One PIRS member said she felt as if she had been touched twice on the hand after asking the spirit of the little girl to do so. Revitalized, we continued the investigation for a few more hours until all activity had ceased. We went home, eager to review the hours of video, audio, and photographs we'd collected.

I was particularly disappointed to discover that the infrared camera, which had been aimed directly at the stage when I saw what looked to be the little girl, had captured nothing but my startled reaction. Perhaps it was just my imagination? We ended up with nothing anomalous on video or audio, and most photographs only captured an occasional speck of dust.

Just when it seemed as if the ghosts of the Schauer Center had alluded us, PIRS-er Walter Skilling found a photograph containing a transparent, misty form with human characteristics. The photo was taken roughly twenty feet from the upstairs elevator near the art gallery. While it's hardly definitive proof of life after death, it certainly is worth sharing.

While I was unable to validate any of the tragic deaths rumored to have occurred in the old cannery decades earlier, the ghostly trio's origins are real to the residents of Hartford, and their presence remains constant at the Schauer.

Image courtesy of Walter Skilling of PIRS.

Directions

From Milwaukee and Fond du Lac: Take HWY 41 to Slinger. Exit at HWY 60, and head west.

From Madison: Take HWY 151 to Columbus. Exit at HWY 60, and follow it east.

In Hartford: From HWY 60, turn north onto Rural Street. The center is on the left.

Section II: Central Washington County

Jackson: County Road P

As I write this, hitchhiking is still sort of legal in Wisconsin, though most people advise against it. I doubt if anyone reading this hasn't heard at least one story about something monstrous happening to either a motorist or a hitchhiker because of this practice, be it true or otherwise.

One such legend exists in Washington County. A stretch of County Road P located between Hasmer Lake and Washington County Fair Park is rumored to be frequented by the ghost of a man who didn't heed society's collective advice.

A man found himself stranded at Washington County Fair Park following a concert one summer night. That Fair Park is involved in this story illustrates that this legend, or at least this version of it, is rather new. The current Fair Park didn't open until the summer of 1999.

He started his nearly three-mile nocturnal walk back to Jackson all the while trying to thumb a ride. Frustration soon set in. In an attempt to get the attention of the seemingly oblivious motorists, he moved too close to traffic. He was fatally struck by a passing car. The negligent driver, in fear of the consequences of what he'd done, sped away from the scene.

The man lay in a ditch for a number of days until the overwhelming smell finally caught the attention of passing motorists. A county road crew investigated, anticipating the carcass of a deer. Instead, what they found was the man's severely decomposed corpse.

Since then, people have reported seeing a man's apparition walking along County Road P. Some have seen him leaning against road signs, weary from his nightly journey, trapped in a perpetual trek home. Interestingly enough, I've yet to hear of anyone seeing this ghost thumbing for a ride. Perhaps he learned his lesson the hard way?

Directions

From Milwaukee: Take HWY 41/45 to Jackson. Exit at HWY 60, and head east.

From Fond du Lac: Take HWY 41 to Slinger. Exit at HWY 60, and head east.

From Madison: Take HWY 151 to Columbus. Exit at HWY 60, and follow it east.

Once in Jackson: From HWY 60, turn north onto CTY P, and head north to CTY PV.

Section II: Central Washington County

Jackson: Hasmer Lake

Surrounded by weeping willows and dotted with lily pads in summer, lovely Hasmer Lake is just outside of Jackson. The lake, which is only fifteen acres around and thirty-four feet deep, is a popular fishing destination despite its small size.

Some longtime residents of Jackson will tell you that it may be a bit deeper than that, though. In fact, some will tell you Hasmer Lake's depths cannot be measured.

The legend of Hasmer Lake is usually set in the 1940s. One sunny day in early spring, a farmer was crossing the lake in a horse-drawn wagon. The yearly thaw was further along than the farmer anticipated, and the ice had grown thin.

As the unsuspecting man got to the middle of the lake, the ice began to crack. He urged his horses forward, but the surface shattered and the farmer and his wagon plunged into the icy water, dragging the horses with it. The lake swallowed them. Divers searched, but no trace of the man, his wagon, or the horses was found. One version of the legend states that one of the divers was consumed by the lake as well.

The idea of a bottomless lake is pretty incredible. One county resident I asked about the legend remarked, "If there's no bottom, what keeps the water in?" A valid question, I'll give him that.

Not long after, I was thumbing through the book *The History of Jackson, Wisconsin (1843–1976)* and found a small paragraph on the Hasmer controversy. Apparently, the property's owner, Peter Hasmer, did lose two horses during an ice harvest, but in 1920. The animals bobbed in the water overnight until they could be dragged from the partially frozen lake by another horse team. The story continues that one and one-half of the horses were buried on Peter Hasmer's property. The missing horse half was fed to the chickens, if you were wondering. So much for the legend of Hasmer, right? Well, maybe not.

One gentleman who's lived in the Jackson area some ninety-seven years recalls two horse-drawn sleds falling into the lake during an ice harvest. He said neither the horse teams nor the sleds were ever found. While he would have been just a boy when the 1920 accident occurred, his recollection shouldn't be dismissed. The gentleman concluded by saying Jackson residents still shy away from swimming in Hasmer.

While it is unlikely that Hasmer Lake is bottomless, given my propensity to sink like a stone, I'll be staying away from it just to be on the safe side.

Directions

From Milwaukee: Take HWY 41/45 to Jackson. Exit at HWY 60, and head east.

From Fond du Lac: Take HWY 41 to Slinger. Exit at HWY 60, and head east.

From Madison: Take HWY 151 to Columbus. Exit at HWY 60, and follow it east.

Once in Jackson: From HWY 60, turn north onto CTY P. The public access driveway to Hasmer Lake is ahead about a tenth of a mile on the right.

Section II: Central Washington County

Jackson: Jackson Marsh

The Jackson Marsh is a 2,300-acre state natural area providing various recreation opportunities, such as hiking, hunting, and bird-watching. The marsh is noteworthy for several reasons, but I'll focus on two.

First, it's a white cedar-tamarack swamp of the variety most commonly found in northern Wisconsin. You'll not find a place like the Jackson Marsh anywhere else in the southeastern portion of the state. Second, if you're to believe the kids in and around Jackson, this is the second of three locations that the Goat Man calls home (see "Goat Man Road" in section 1 and "Hogsback Road" in section 3). While I'm not certain which of the two Goat Man legends is applicable to this location, the thought of running into a bloodthirsty satyr in the middle of the swamp is an unappealing idea regardless.

If you're roaming around the marsh looking for such rare wildlife as the state-threatened Kentucky warbler, be cautious. The Goat Man could be lurking in the next tract of silver maples.

Directions

From Milwaukee: Take HWY 41/45 to Jackson. Exit at HWY 60, and head east.

From Fond du Lac: Take HWY 41 to Slinger. Exit at HWY 60, and head east.

From Madison: Take HWY 151 to Columbus. Exit at HWY 60, and follow it east.

Once in Jackson: From HWY 60, turn north onto Division Road/CTY G. The public access to the marsh is ahead about a mile on the left.

Section II: Central Washington County

Polk: Cedar Creek Cemetery

Stories about an evil witch and a curse from beyond the grave are what legend trippers like me live for. I was following Alan Gee and Dan Cartwright of the Wisconsin Area Paranormal Society (WAPS) around Washington County on a soggy, stormy August Saturday morning when I first heard about the witch's grave at Cedar Creek Cemetery (alternatively known as Maxon Cemetery) in the town of Polk. Alan and Dan, who both grew up in nearby West Bend, jumped at the chance to show me many of the locations they used to legend-trip as teens.

I first heard the details of the legend while I was standing in the cemetery itself. Thunder was crashing off in the distance, and the rain began falling lightly enough for a swarm of voracious mosquitos to take flight. Apparently, none of them had had a chance to feed in several days, years perhaps, judging from their relentless attack.

The legend of the witch's curse is incredibly vague, as most legends are. Supposedly, an old woman suspected of practicing the dark arts was buried near the front of the cemetery. She was given a large rock, which supposedly bears a pentagram, as a crude tombstone. Once the symbol is worn away by time and the elements, the old witch will return and walk the earth. Dan, now middle-aged, remembers coming to the cemetery in his youth and finding the grave of the witch, complete with pentagram.

We wandered through the cemetery in search of the grave but had no luck finding it. After nearly a half hour of mounting frustration and mosquito bites, I finally found a badly deteriorated stone bearing the Masonic "square and compasses" symbol. It's possible that someone seeing this stone on a moonlit night could interpret it as a pentagram, especially in a deserted country cemetery. Dan wasn't convinced. The masonic tombstone was located in the wrong part of the cemetery, he said.

The storm was moving closer, and we were losing blood quickly. We called off the search, having wandered through most of the small old cemetery anyway.

There's a lot in the legend of the witch's grave that leads me to believe it's likely just a legend. Would a suspected witch be buried right at the entrance of the cemetery, especially with a pentagram marking her burial? I suppose the pentagram could have been added later as an act of vandalism, but supposing doesn't solve mysteries.

Later that week, I was discussing the trip with my friend Mike, a fellow legend-trip enthusiast. He'd never heard the legend, but he'd had his own experience at the cemetery. He and a friend were making a homemade horror movie and went out to film in the cemetery.

"I was running the camera, moving from right to left, and panning back to center. After a couple of days, I went over the footage, and while viewing the panning-over shot, there was a bench up against the fence on the north side. There were two children, a boy and a girl, probably between the ages of six and ten years old, clowning around on the bench. They were wearing clothing from the late 1800s or maybe the early 1900s. The problem with this is we were the only two people there. I think I still have the footage somewhere in a box packed away."

So far, the footage hasn't been found, much to Mike's regret. It probably slipped into another dimension along with an infamous photo from my childhood that apparently contained an image of my grandfather's ghost. How I wish Grandma hadn't lost that photo. It often seems evidence of the paranormal is as elusive as the phenomena themselves.

After hearing Mike's story, I went back to the cemetery, this time armed with bug spray, and looked around again. I combed the entire cemetery twice over. I never located the witch's grave, which means that either the stone was removed, it never existed, or the symbol wore away and the witch has returned. If she is back, I'm certain she isn't lingering in Cedar Creek Cemetery.

Walking through the cemetery alone, unburdened by fear of mosquitos or lightning strikes, I found the place overwhelmingly peaceful. If there are ghosts there, they're likely small children laughing and playing. There's nothing to be afraid of. I often find myself thinking about those two small children, playing for all eternity. I'll likely never know their identities; I'm just glad they're happy.

Section II: Central Washington County

Directions

From Milwaukee: Take HWY 41/45 to Jackson. Exit at HWY 60, and head west.

From Fond du Lac: Take HWY 41 to Slinger. Exit at HWY 60, and head east.

From Madison: Take HWY 151 to Columbus. Exit at HWY 60, and follow it east.

Once in Jackson: From HWY 60, turn north onto Lily Road. At CTY C/Cedar Creek Road, Lily Road becomes CTY Z. Follow CTY Z. The cemetery is ahead about a half mile on the right.

Slinger:
The Elementary School and High School

Since you're reading a book like this, I'd be very surprised if you've not seen the 1982 blockbuster film *Poltergeist*, but I feel obligated to summarize it anyway. Be warned though, a spoiler approaches.

In the film, a family begins to experience paranormal activity in their home. What starts out as a harmless novelty quickly escalates into the abduction of the family's young daughter and a full-blown supernatural assault. The family discovers that their neighborhood was built over a cemetery, and to save money, the developers had moved only the tombstones—not the bodies. While this film didn't invent the idea that grave desecration can awaken spirits, it certainly embedded it in the imagination of America. Nowadays, nearly any structure built over a human burial has quickly earned a paranormal reputation. This is true for Slinger Elementary School, where there are still tombstones located on the property.

The Elementary School

In 1969, the school needed to expand. Land was purchased from the nearby St. John's United Church of Christ. The church's cemetery, which had a history dating back to the 1800s, was on land that was part of the purchase. As part of the agreement made with descendants of the interred, the bodies were removed, but the tombstones remained behind, arranged together in a landscaped area complete with a commemorative sign. The school's addition was built over the former cemetery.

Section II: Central Washington County

As the Internet became a part of everyday life, the school soon began to appear on paranormal websites. In 2003, a *Milwaukee Journal-Sentinel* article investigated the rumors. Then Slinger School District administrator Joe Wikrent denied that there had been any haunting and stated that all bodies had been relocated. Wikrent was a teacher at the nearby high school and recalls all the bodies being moved.

While there is no way to be absolutely certain some unmarked grave wasn't overlooked, it doesn't seem to matter. Wikrent's statements apparently were enough to keep any of the rumors from gaining a foothold. When I tried to follow old links to information about the alleged haunting, all I could find were frustrating "404 Page Not Found" error screens. When I asked longtime Slinger residents about the alleged haunting—and I asked many—none had ever heard of any ghosts at the elementary school. Slinger High School, which is located across the parking lot, is a different story.

The High School

For a large segment of the population, high school was a numbing blur of cliques, bullying, and gym class—a true nightmare. No need for demons or monsters, these real-world traumas are plenty to keep the average youth awake at night. But what if, on top of all this, you have to worry about ghosts? One reader-submitted article titled *Haunted High School* on Ghostvillage.com tells a story from 1987 in which the writer and a group of his friends were chased away from the school by the ghost of a former student.

The ghost supposedly belonged to a young man who was allegedly killed during gym class by a shot put and now spends the afterlife trapped on the school grounds. According to the story, they heard the sound of running coming from the gymnasium. The sound grew nearer until finally the door they stood near burst open from a blast of cold wind. The article also states that members of the janitorial staff frequently feel as if they are being followed and that they, too, experienced doors opening and closing seemingly by themselves.

At least two student have died at Slinger High School, though not the current high school, which was built in 1964. Both incidents occurred at the old high school, which is now Slinger Elementary School next door.

Thanks to a Richfield Historical Society newsletter, I learned the infamous shot-put incident took place in 1946. A fourteen-year-old student by the last name of Lofy was struck in the head. He passed away ten days later.

This unfortunate fellow isn't the only possible culprit behind the activity. I learned of a second death from a Washington County Historical Society volunteer, whose classmate had been killed by lightning.

"I believe it happened in the spring of 1959. I know I was in third grade. The boy who was electrocuted was named Zelm. The location was on the playground close to where the front entrance is for the high school today. The sky was a green color [so] the teacher called us in early. Our class was already inside when lightning struck him. When we got to our classroom, all the blinds were down."

While I have no clue if either school is haunted, it is very rewarding to prove that there is some truth to any legend.

One Slinger High alumnus I spoke with, who wishes to remain anonymous, was unaware of the haunting, but he did offer a rather humorous theory behind any paranormal activity at the current high school.

"[A teacher I had] was in her eighties when I took her class in the late 1980s. She always said she would come back and haunt all of us bad kids who tormented her. She had brandy and whiskey in her desk drawer and was always taking a swig, then [she'd] fall asleep during class."

I include this as a valuable lesson to any kids reading this: always be kind to your teachers; otherwise, you yourself could be the cause of a haunting.

Directions

From Milwaukee and Fond du Lac: Take HWY 41 to Slinger. Exit at HWY 60, and head west.

From Madison: Take HWY 151 to Columbus. Exit at HWY 60, and follow it east.

Once in Slinger: From HWY 60, turn north onto E Washington Street. Turn left onto Beine Street. The schools are straight ahead.

Section III: Southern Washington County

Erin: Holy Hill

You don't have to be Catholic, or even Christian, to gaze up at Holy Hill and feel a spiritual power. The current building atop Holy Hill is an awe-inspiring dual-spired chapel shrine with the rather wordy name "the Basilica of the National Shrine of Mary, Help of Christians, at Holy Hill." Most folks keep it whittled down to "Holy Hill," though.

Literally thousands of faithful from all corners of the world travel yearly to the shrine chapel. Many visit not only to take in the beauty of the area, which would be enough of a reason for most, but also to be healed. Just outside the chapel door is a collection of crutches, braces, and wheelchairs left behind by pilgrims who were miraculously cured.

The legend of Holy Hill began well before the state of Wisconsin even existed. Native Americans long considered the hill, which is really a glacially formed moulin kame, as a sacred place, and they'd climb it to worship.

Christians first laid claim to the hill in the 1670s. A mysterious Jesuit missionary supposedly came to the hill and planted a cross in the name of Mary, proclaiming it forever a holy place. Potawatomi and Menomonee legends do tell of this "black-robed chief," who came from Lake Michigan.

A diary and a parchment map left by the missionary were found by a French monk working in Quebec, Canada. That this monk's name was François Soubrio and that he became known as "the Hermit of Holy Hill" is about all the historians can agree upon. One version of his life paints him as a mere religious eccentric, another as a murderer seeking forgiveness. Given the nature of this book, we'll focus on the latter.

According to the book *Miracle Hill: A Legendary Tale of Wisconsin* by William Ayres Armstrong, soon after François began his education for the priesthood, he fell in love with a young woman. He strayed from his sacred vows by asking her to be his wife. The ensuing scandal disgraced him in the eyes of both his family and the church. François went into self-imposed exile to test the strength of their love. He returned after two years to find his fiancée had betrayed him for another man. He killed her and fled to Canada where he became a monk.

Moved by the description of Holy Hill he'd stumbled upon, he vowed to find it and plant the cross there once more. Along the way, he became so ill that he lost the use of his legs. Finally though, François dragged himself to the top of Holy Hill. He prayed all through the night, and when dawn broke, he was cured.

Image courtesy of Washington County Historical Society.

Soon after, his presence became known. Rumor of the healing spread across the countryside. People helped build a cabin for the man who'd previously been living in a dugout on the hill.

The third and current chapel shrine on Holy Hill was built in 1926 and is now listed on the National and State Registers of Historic Places. When you visit, be sure to climb the scenic tower, which is nearly 1500 feet above sea level. Be aware that the tower is closed from November 1 until May 1 and also closes for inclement weather.

Directions

From Milwaukee and Fond du Lac: Take HWY 41 to Richfield. Exit at HWY 167 W/Holy Hill Road, and head west.

From Madison: Take HWY 151 to Columbus. Exit at HWY 60, and follow it east. Turn south onto HWY 83/S Main Street. Follow HWY 83. Turn left onto HWY 167/Holy Hill Road.

Once in Erin: The basilica is on the south side of the road; watch for the signs.

Section III: Southern Washington County

Erin: State Highway 167

Ever hear of something called the bearwolf? If you haven't, don't worry; you're in the majority. The bearwolf is a bizarre, absolutely sensational cryptid that was first seen in Washington County near Holy Hill back in 2006, and hardly anyone knows about it.

How could anyone be oblivious to a seven-foot-tall, sometimes bipedal creature with a body like a bear and a head like a wolf stalking through the kames and eskers near their homes? Probably because when DNR employee Steve Krueger reported his startling encounter with this puzzling amalgamation, a confused—or amused—Washington County sheriff's deputy identified the creature as a "yeti" in the police report. A plethora of news outlets labeled the creature "bigfoot" and created a media blitz.

The Krueger sighting is covered in great detail in Linda Godfrey's book *Strange Wisconsin: More Badger State Weirdness*, along with other sightings near Holy Hill. Godfrey interviewed Krueger during the Holy Hill "bigfoot" frenzy and is the leading expert in unknown canine sightings in the United States. Linda has written books about the Michigan Dog Man and the infamous Wisconsin werewolf, the Beast of Bray Road. In fact, it was Godfrey who linked Krueger's sighting of "something like a bear" to the bearwolf, a cryptid previously witnessed near Wausau, Wisconsin.

According to Godfrey's book, Krueger was driving down State Highway 167 east of Holy Hill at 1:30 a.m. collecting roadkill when he saw a dead deer on the side of the road not marked for pickup. He stopped and hoisted it onto his truck anyway. While he was filling out paperwork, his vehicle began to shake. He looked into his rearview mirror and saw a large, six or seven-foot-tall creature, covered in black fur with a canine-like head, reaching into the back of his truck. Krueger panicked and sped away as the creature dragged the deer back into the road, snagging an aluminum ramp as well.

After a few minutes, Krueger calmed down and returned to retrieve the ramp. The creature, the deer carcass, and the ramp had all vanished. He spent the rest of the night debating whether or not he should tell anyone what had happened. Deciding that the creature might be dangerous, he alerted the police. Krueger later remarked to Godfrey that he wished he'd never told anyone of the sighting because of all the publicity it received.

Out of respect, I decided not to contact Krueger. Instead, I went seeking anyone else who might have seen this unusual scavenger.

Other Sightings and Possible Explanations

After posting several queries on the Internet, I received an e-mail from a woman whom I'll call A.J.

> In June 2006, we lived by the YMCA on Highway 33 in West Bend.
>
> My two sons and their buddy saw a fox or cat running like mad into the swamp and gave chase. They came upon a hairy animal in the woods that looked like a dog but had no tail and was on two legs. It was furry and had red eyes.
>
> It was eating the animal they had been chasing. They said they were not afraid of the creature. It did not seem to want to hurt them, but it looked them in the eyes. They came into the house yelling and told me about this. They said it was "a *lot* bigger than Grandpa." My father was six-four.
>
> I did not believe them. I told them it was just someone in a fur coat. Shortly after this, I saw [the Krueger Holy Hill sighting] on the news that described the same thing the boys had seen. I knew then what they saw.

So what exactly is a bearwolf, and where did it come from? Some cryptozoologists think it's an undiscovered species of bruin or canine. Some ghost hunters believe it's an elemental—a nature spirit—given how frequently it and creatures similar to it are seen near sacred Native American lands (see Lizard Mound County Park in section 1). Skeptics think it's a misidentified bear. Animals once banished to the northern portion of the state, such as gray wolves and black bear, have experienced population booms in recent decades and are moving south in search of new territory. An August 2011 *Milwaukee Magazine* article by Kurt Chandler uses a 2010 Port Washington black bear scare to illustrate this southern migration. The bear, which had been spotted days earlier in Washington County near Kewaskum, appeared near downtown Port Washington during a crowded festival. The bear treed itself, and it was eventually tranquilized and relocated to a safer place, much to everyone's relief, especially the bear's. Out of all three possible explanations, a misidentified bear seems most likely. Yet, in every instance I've read about, bearwolf witnesses have claimed familiarity with bears and are positive what they saw wasn't a bear. In the case of A.J.'s sons' story, bears certainly do not have red eyes.

While the bearwolf has been pretty quiet in recent years, I heard rumors of a sighting in Kewaskum in the spring of 2012. A large black animal was seen standing on all fours eating a dead turkey on Highway 45. Alarmed motorists slammed on their brakes to avoid hitting the animal, which ran away on two legs. Unfortunately, I've been unable to speak with any of the witnesses, so as of now, this story is merely gossip.

Cryptid, nature spirit, bear—whatever it is—if you see the bearwolf, you automatically win the Legend Tripper's Lifetime Achievement Award. This prestigious award is merely honorary, but it does include a complimentary debriefing from this writer—not to be confused with a depantsing, mind you.

Directions

From Milwaukee and Fond du Lac: Take HWY 41 to Richfield. Exit at HWY 167 W/Holy Hill Road, and head west.

From Madison: Take HWY 151 to Columbus. Exit at HWY 60, and follow it east. Turn south onto HWY 83/S Main Street. Follow HWY 83. Turn left onto HWY 167/Holy Hill Road.

Once in Erin: The area where the bearwolf has been sighted is between HWY 164 and CTY K along HWY 167/Holy Hill Road.

Erin: Tally Ho Pub and Grill

The most commonly accepted catalyst for a haunting is a violent death, such as murder. Compound this atrocious crime with an unconsecrated burial, and you have all the ingredients for trouble. This exact recipe is found at the Tally Ho Pub and Grill in Erin, which was established in the 1800s as a hotel, saloon, and general store.

According to owner Chaz Hastings, the restaurant hosts an often friendly, but sometimes violent, poltergeist. The entity is thought to be Emily Rattenbach, who lived from 1905 until 1936. Emily's parents owned the establishment in the 1930s, when the building functioned as a brothel. According to tradition, Emily's father was a violent alcoholic who put her to work serving up more than just drinks. Legend says she was murdered, and her body was buried in the basement and covered with large stones.

Though Emily's apparition has been seen on occasion as a lady in white, she most often passes unseen, her presence given away by the scent of lavender and lemon balm.

Emily's antics are usually harmless. Doors open and close by themselves, unexplained voices are heard after bar close, and footsteps follow you through dark basement hallways—unnerving, yes, but hardly life threatening. However, when an employee comes along whom Emily doesn't seem to like, she can be quite vicious.

On two different occasions, cooks have been injured when a large kitchen knife inexplicably flew off a magnetic strip above the kitchen sink. On both occasions, stitches were required.

One employee, who lives above the bar, is a favorite target of Emily. His bed covers are stripped off him in the middle of the night, and his possessions routinely disappear, never to be seen again.

Interestingly, all of the employees who have been tormented are male. It seems natural that the ghost of an alleged murdered prostitute with an abusive father would have issues with men.

"If you're nice to her, she's nice to you. She doesn't like to be cursed at. When you do that, that's when she takes your things," said a waitress, when asked about Emily's mood swings.

Image courtesy of Washington County Historical Society.

Armed with this information, I was asked to return with the Paranormal Investigation and Research Society (PIRS) to investigate. On our first visit, we wanted to get a feel for the location, and I had a rather interesting personal experience in the basement where Emily is supposedly buried.

The owner's young son told us that he would often hear footsteps following him through the basement corridors. He and I were standing in the basement hallway in complete darkness when we heard an unknown, grinding noise several feet away near Emily's rumored grave. I called out and got no answer. I turned on my flashlight, and we made our way down the hallway toward the noise. When we reached the location, we heard the sound again, this time under our own feet. The corridor was covered in a fine dusting of broken glass. Had we heard Emily's footsteps?

PIRS made arrangements to return in a few weeks after bar close, so we could collect evidence without the possibility of contamination by the mortal merrymaking upstairs.

After we had completed our preliminary investigation, the gentleman who lives upstairs met us in the parking lot. He'd expected us to stay much later and had missed the whole affair. Nearly in tears, he told us about numerous expensive belongings that had gone missing, all of which he blamed on Emily. He considered himself to be at the center of the activity and wanted us to help him. In the spirit of kindness, we asked him to be present for the next investigation.

When PIRS arrived the second time, we brought along all of our equipment, including a full DVR system with audio and night-vision capabilities.

The only Tally Ho staff members present were a bartender and the gentleman being targeted by Emily. He was still very emotional. He was adamant that we make some sort of contact with her, to validate his experiences. He'd insisted that he be allowed to provoke Emily, which goes against PIRS policy. While that might seem a good idea, since she supposedly responds to negative stimulation, we were only there for a very short time, and if we angered an entity, we weren't the ones who would have to live with the consequences. We explained this to the man, but he kept his resolve.

Things got interesting before we had even finished setting up. I went down into the basement to aim one of our night-vision cameras, and the gentleman went down with me. While I was straightening the camera, he began insulting and threatening Emily. I asked him to settle down since the investigation hadn't started yet. He stomped around the corner into a part of the basement used for food storage. A bit exasperated, I finished my chore. There was a loud thud, and the gentleman screamed. He ran around the corner terrified and asked me to bring a camera.

I reluctantly followed him. Lying on the floor several feet from a shelf was a smashed gallon jar of mayonnaise. He told me that it had flown off the shelf as he provoked the ghost. If this was true, it would have been amazing evidence. However, since he was the only one who had witnessed it and he didn't have a camera, we couldn't consider it reliable. I snapped a picture, but a photograph of spilled mayo isn't proof of life after death. There's no way to prove he hadn't simply accidentally knocked it over on his own given his agitated state. I took him back upstairs, and we explained to him how extremely important it was that he not wander off on his own.

After the situation calmed down, we began our investigation. The group took turns investigating various parts of the building. About a half an hour into the investigation, PIRS founders Kellie Wirtz and Mike

Section III: Southern Washington County

Hoke called down to the bar area where I was monitoring the DVR system. They had been investigating the upstairs banquet room when they'd heard water flowing in the bathroom. Upon opening the door, they'd found the faucet running unattended. Two other PIRS investigators had just been upstairs conducting an EVP session, so I checked with them and neither had used the restroom or heard water. The bartender had told us the room hadn't been used in several days, and staff never went up there without cause, especially since Emily had recently been blamed for throwing a child's booster seat upstairs. While it's unlikely the water had been running earlier when our previous group was upstairs, it is possible that it was. No one had witnessed the faucet go on by itself, and we had no camera in the bathroom. We once again had to toss out what would have been amazing evidence.

As the night progressed, activity seemed to cease. We'd been in every part of the building in nearly every possible combination. I paired up with another PIRS member and decided to go into the basement one more time. Earlier in the evening, I'd conducted an EVP session by Emily's alleged grave and thought I'd seen an orb of red light travel up the cooler toward the basement ceiling, and I couldn't get it out of my mind. We walked past the overturned jar of mayo, now pungent in the warm, damp basement air.

My companion noticed that the atmosphere seemed different in the basement from what it had been earlier in the night. I agreed. It felt heavier. As we concluded an EVP session, I heard the same gritty noise I'd heard on our initial visit, as though someone were walking on broken glass. I called out, and no one replied. We quickly walked toward the glass on the floor but found no one. We began another EVP session at Emily's legendary grave. I was pleading with her to make herself known to us. In the end, she didn't manifest. She seemed to have been playing with us all night, making her presence known, but not allowing us to prove it.

We returned to the bar. I sat on a bar stool monitoring the DVR system with the gentleman Emily had been targeting. Glancing around the bar, I noticed the various religious relics and Irish Catholic imagery that filled nearly every available space of the barroom and dining area. It occurred to me that, beyond the accusation that Emily had thrown a child seat in the banquet room, all her hijinks occurred in areas of the building lacking these Christian totems: the basement,

the kitchen, and the gentleman's upstairs apartment. I advised him that perhaps the religious icons in the pub comforted Emily and suggested maybe if he decorated his apartment similarly, she'd leave him be. He said nothing. A while later, the other PIRS-ers returned from the basement. Not so much as a disembodied footstep from Emily. We packed up our gear and started home just before dawn, excited, tired, and frustrated.

The last time I spoke with the folks at the Tally Ho, they told me the upstairs tenant had decided to call it quits and find a new apartment. No word on if he ever took my advice. The rest of those at the Tally Ho still believe Emily is haunting the pub, but no one seems to mind it. They trust that as long as they treat her with respect, she'll continue to keep her activity reduced to an occasional noise in the darkness. The general consensus at the Tally Ho seems to be, "Emily, please don't scare us!"

Directions

From Milwaukee and Fond du Lac: Take HWY 41 to Richfield. Exit at HWY 167 W/Holy Hill Road, and head west. Turn north onto HWY 83. The restaurant is ahead about half a mile on the left.

From Madison: Take HWY 151 to Columbus. Exit at HWY 60, and follow it east. Turn south onto HWY 83/S Main Street. Follow HWY 83. The restaurant is on the right.

Section III: Southern Washington County

Germantown: Berg's Saloon

Every now and then, you find a pub you just don't want to leave. Evidently, Berg's Saloon is just such a pub. Originally built in the 1880s, the saloon has had a bevy of names, including the Yesterday Tavern, the Longhorn Inn, and its present identity, RT Sports Corner.

Despite the frequent name changes, Germantown residents will likely always know it as Berg's Saloon. In fact, the pub's founder, John Berg, is often accused of being one of the spooks behind the pub's haunting, at least according to a 1984 *Milwaukee Journal* article. "Grand Pa" John Berg was cutting ice from a nearby creek one frigid winter's day when the ice cracked, sending him tumbling through. Though he pulled himself out of the numbing water, a few weeks later, he succumbed to pneumonia and was interred across the street from his saloon, at Christ Church's Pioneer Cemetery.

John Berg has been seen at his beloved saloon at least once since his passing. A former owner, whose identity has been lost to decades of beery retellings, once heard a ruckus just past closing. The owner saw an old, white-haired man dropping beer mugs behind the bar. The owner charged the rather frail-looking stranger and ended up grabbing only empty air, a pile of broken glass at his feet. Later, the owner identified the vanishing vandal as John Berg, whose photo once hung on the wall.

Another suspected ghost is identified only as Ray. Ray owned the saloon when it was known as the Longhorn Inn. His specter has been blamed for knocking over bar stools, leaving cold beers on the bar past close, and turning hot dogs on the grill.

These days, if either John or Ray still visit their former—or current—haunt, the folks at RT Sports Corner don't seem to be making much noise about it. I was unable to speak with the saloon's current owners, but I was able to talk to one bartender. When asked if the haunting was something that the current owners talked about, she simply replied, "Not around me they don't."

Image courtesy of Washington County Historical Society.

Directions

From Milwaukee and Fond du Lac: Take HWY 41 to Richfield. Exit at HWY 167 W/Holy Hill Road, and head east on Holy Hill Road.

From Madison: Take HWY 151 to Columbus. Exit at HWY 60, and follow it east. Take HWY 41 south to Richfield. Exit at HWY 167 W/Holy Hill Road, and head east on Holy Hill Road.

Once in Germantown: From the six-way intersection of Holy Hill Road, HWY 145/Fond du Lac Avenue, and Maple Road, follow Holy Hill Road east. The restaurant is on the right.

Section III: Southern Washington County

Germantown: Dheinsville Settlement Park Intersection

Dheinsville has the distinction of being the first commercial business district in the township of Germantown. In 1842, the Dhein family purchased eight hundred acres of land for themselves and several other families; they were all from Siedersbach, Germany.

The settlers spent their first night in Dheinsville in a hastily made lean-to. The Dheins quickly befriended the Native Americans in the area and went to work constructing homes.

On May 12, 1843, Phillip Dhein Jr. became the first European born in the wilderness of Washington County, firmly establishing Dheinsville.

Nearly 170 years since it was settled, Dheinsville hasn't grown much. The little settlement occupies only a handful of square blocks around the intersection of Holy Hill Road, Maple Road, and Fond Du Lac Avenue, a dangerous six-way intersection that's said to be frequented by a ghost, according to numerous Internet posts.

Many times, the figure of a man has been seen in or near the intersection waving to traffic. He's been known to be so distracting that he's caused motorists to drive into ditches. When the perplexed and often infuriated drivers return to where they saw the figure, no one is there.

On an exquisite August day, I decided to drive to Settlement Park and talk to the folks at the Germantown Historical Society. The society operates the Bast Bell Museum, the Valentine Wolf Haus Museum and Research Center, and the Christ Church Museum of Local History, all of which are located in Settlement Park. The society employee I spoke with was unfamiliar with the haunting, though he did comment on how awful the intersection is.

"A lot of times, when I leave [the Bast Bell Museum] on weekend afternoons, I'll have to drive past cars that are piled up out here. Cops and ambulances and everything all over the place."

Perhaps the ghost doesn't mean to cause carnage. Could it be he's simply trying to warn drivers of the dangerous intersection they're approaching?

Or maybe he's a confused spirit from nearby Christ Church's Pioneer Cemetery looking for a ride home? Could it be "Grand Pa" John Berg, the ghostly personality from nearby Berg's Saloon? Mr. Berg is buried in the cemetery by the intersection.

No matter the identity of the intersection's ghost, please proceed with caution when driving through Dheinsville. A legend trip ending in a smashed-up vehicle is a poor legend trip, indeed. It should be mentioned the Germantown Historical Society offers a historic walking tour of Dheinsville Settlement Park. While the tour doesn't offer any paranormal content, perhaps you'll luck out and catch a glimpse of a ghost waving from the crossroads.

Directions

From Milwaukee and Fond du Lac: Take HWY 41 to Richfield. Exit at HWY 167 W/Holy Hill Road, and head east on Holy Hill Road.

From Madison: Take HWY 151 to Columbus. Exit at HWY 60, and follow it east. Take HWY 41 south to Richfield. Exit at HWY 167 W/Holy Hill Road, and head east on Holy Hill Road.

Once in Germantown: From the six-way intersection of Holy Hill Road, HWY 145/Fond du Lac Avenue, and Maple Road, follow Holy Hill Road east. The settlement is on the left.

Section III: Southern Washington County

Germantown: Madam Belle's Silver Dollar Saloon

When they hear the word *Wisconsin*, most people are reminded of cheese, the Green Bay Packers, snow—and if you're the type who reads books like this—Ed Gein. What most people don't think about are gangsters. Wisconsin's close proximity to Chicago made the state a popular retreat for the Windy City's heavy hitters during the Prohibition Era, from 1920 to 1933.

Some would expect notorious outlaws to stick to heavily populated areas like Milwaukee or Madison. Not so. Small towns all over Wisconsin have had brushes with Chi-Town's bootlegging bad boys, even quiet little slices of Washington County have legends involving organized crime. Madam Belle's Silver Dollar Saloon is at the center of just such a legend. If the stories are true, Belle's used to serve up more than just good food during America's "noble experiment" of banning alcohol. The building was once an oasis of bathtub gin and ladies of ill repute.

"You can really tell the place used to be a brothel when you go upstairs. There are several small, ten-feet-by-ten-feet rooms that used to be used by the women," says Jason Pipkorn, one of the saloon's current owners.

Al Capone is rumored to have frequented the place, buying his cronies time with the girls. Two holes still scar the wall from bullets supposedly fired by Capone himself. When I heard the place might be haunted, my mind immediately conjured up scenarios involving Alphonse himself in a sharp-looking, but translucent, pin-striped suit, walking silently through the saloon after bar close.

When Jason told me the type of phenomena experienced, it seems much more likely that the resident ghost is Madam Belle herself.

"When people are working down in the basement, they will hear the bell over the bar ringing. Sometimes, when they've come up to investigate, the bell is moving like it just rang."

And what exactly is the significance of that bell anyway? Jason tells us the colorful, all right, *blue* legend of Madam Belle.

"They say she wouldn't wear any undergarments under her dress. If someone tipped her enough, she'd hop onto the bar and kick the bell."

So is Madam Belle really still high kicking after all these years? Perhaps. In addition to phantom taps and shoves, employees glimpse apparitions in their peripheral vision.

One employee by the name of Jammi got a better look than most after clearing out the saloon and locking up for the night. While working behind the bar, she said she saw a young woman, about thirty years old, with dark hair wearing loose-fitting black clothing, who quickly vanished.

I asked Jason if he thought Belle's is haunted.

"I've had nothing happen to me, but there are way too many stories for it not to be."

After the interview, Jason insisted that I see the saloon for myself.

"You need to stop by some night and get a feel for the place and its history. It was a real dump when we bought it. Ugly drop ceilings, it was awful. We fixed it up."

I wondered if perhaps this remodeling could be responsible for the recent sightings of Belle's Lady in Black.

When I arrived, it was obvious the current ownership wasn't just open about the saloon's wild past but actively embraces it. A sign reading "Beware: Pickpockets and Loose Women" greeted me at the door. Every surface that wasn't decorated in wanted posters was decorated in vintage T and A. Even the top of the bar was covered with girly girl ads and pub tokens inscribed with double entendres. My favorite read "Good for One Screw—Tombstone, AZ."

Joining me for dinner at Belle's this night were several members of the Paranormal Investigation and Research Society (PIRS), as well as members of the Wisconsin Area Paranormal Society (WAPS). The people at Belle's weren't just willing to talk about their ghost, they would let us come hunt for it as well.

After our meal, Jason arrived and gave us a quick tour of the location. Highlights included the infamous bell, the cellar exit supposedly used by gangsters fleeing federal agents, and the dining room where the Lady in Black has been seen. What immediately caught my attention was that she's often seen within a few feet of an oversized casket adorned with the saloon's name, along with the phrase "Wanted Dead or Alive." Patrons can step inside for a macabre photo op, while giving the saloon some free, viral advertising. I know I couldn't resist doing a few distasteful, but fun, poses. If Belle's does have a ghost, perhaps this gallows humor irks the Lady in Black?

We paranormal investigators spent a long night collecting hours of audio and video footage but had a rather uneventful hunt. After a couple of days of careful analysis, we found some strange light anomalies in photographs, but no Lady in Black and no sounds of phantom bells. We did discover high electromagnetic field (EMF) readings in the vicinity of where the Lady in Black is often seen. Long-term exposure to high EMF can cause feelings of being watched and other reported "ghostly" phenomena. Of course, some say unusual levels of this energy can allow spirits to manifest.

I decided to head to the Washington County Historical Society to see what I could find out about the history of the building. While I was there, a senior volunteer in the research center confided that he attributes the legend of "Madam Belle's" infamous bell kicks to the saloon's former owner Mike Schweitzer and his wife Sybil, also called Belle. In the early 1940s, the place was known as the Silver Dollar Bar. Sybil did use the bell as a way of enticing tips from patrons. Once she'd obtained the desired amount of tips, instead of hoping on the bar, she'd lower the bell—which hung from a rope—to ankle level and deliver a good, swift kick to raucous laughter from an amused, but likely disappointed, crowd. The volunteer wouldn't rule out that she never delivered a high kick from atop the bar, but he did say she likely only did it for "very close friends."

However, other folks I spoke with who lived near the Silver Dollar Bar said that most, if not all, the stories regarding Belle's kicking abilities were true and then some.

While Belle's methods are hotly debated, she did seem to ring that bell quiet often. Was the bar ever a brothel? It probably was at some point. Washington County had a large number of known brothels and speakeasies during Prohibition.

I was unable to find any proof Capone or any of his gangster friends ever set foot in Belle's, but legends of their presence in southeastern Washington County are plentiful. People like Capone didn't advertise their activities, especially at houses of ill repute. One gentleman, who lives near Belle's, does recall a drive-by shooting at the bar in the 1950s. Thankfully, no one was killed.

According to the current owners of the saloon, someone's still ringing that bell, and it could be the Lady in Black. So is this darkly dressed spirit the wife of a former owner? Or an anonymous call girl who ran afoul of the Mob? Maybe it's someone else entirely. It's a mystery that might never be solved.

Directions

From Milwaukee and Fond du Lac: Take HWY 41/45 to Richfield. Exit at HWY 145/Fond du Lac Avenue, and head south. The restaurant is on the right, at the intersection of HWY 145 and Goldenthal Road.

From Madison: Take HWY 151 to Columbus. Exit at HWY 60, and follow it east. Take HWY 41 south to Richfield. Exit at HWY 145/Fond du Lac Avenue, and head south.

Once in Germantown: Follow HWY 145. The restaurant is on the right, at the intersection of HWY 145 and Goldenthal Road.

Section III: Southern Washington County

Germantown: Mary Buth Farm

The Mary Buth Farm has long had a reputation for being haunted. The Buths were among Germantown's original settlers. The family settled the land in the 1830s and resided there until 1923. For decades, the locals have said that Mary Buth and her daughter, confusingly also named Mary, haunt the grounds by day and then retreat into the old farmhouse by night.

The legend of the Mary Buth Farm really gained steam thanks to the book *Haunted Wisconsin* by Michael Normal and Beth Scott. In 1965, the farm was occupied by the Tom Walton Family. Tom was a professor at the University of Wisconsin-Milwaukee. On New Year's Eve that year, various strange phenomena occurred during a party culminating with the appearance of an apparition dressed in black. The living room television lost power, the room grew cold, and the family and their guests saw a figure standing outside, gazing in at them. Before anyone could investigate, she disappeared.

The Waltons asked a psychic and writer by the name of Mary Leader to investigate. After using a Ouija board, Leader claimed the ghosts were in fact the Marys. The elder Mary supposedly haunted the house, while the outside was the domain of her "evil" daughter, who searched for a missing lover. Normal and Scott go on to describe an eerie, classic haunting ripe with disembodied footsteps, unexplainable violin music, and the occasional female apparition vanishing into the mists on the farm property. The Waltons moved away in the late 1970s, and the family that replaced them reported that local kids were scared to come near the property because of its ghosts.

Apparently, the kids in and around Germantown are a lot braver these days. Trespassing on the Buth farm has become a major problem. Online paranormal forums are littered with posts by people who have ventured onto the property hoping to see a ghost. Many confess that their adventure ended with either a citation from police or a trip to jail.

The legend of the Buth haunting has grown progressively more sensational since *Haunted Wisconsin* was first published in 1980. One version of the legend I've read online says that one of the Marys was killed by her husband and buried in the back of the property.

Another states that one of the Marys took to caring for injured Civil War soldiers. She and one of the wounded fell in love and were to be married. On the day of their wedding, her fiancé ran away. She got a bit angry and began murdering the remaining soldiers with an ax until a neighboring farmer shot her dead. The insane ax-wielding Mary apparently also had a dog, which starved itself to death out of grief. If you approach her grave at night, two blood-red eyes will appear, and the beast will growl.

One young man from Germantown I spoke with swears his girlfriend was chased from the property by the gore-covered ghost of one of the women. This is all a touch more unsettling than a woman in black disappearing outside the window, huh?

A *Milwaukee Journal-Sentinel* article from 2000 debunked the story of the scandalous deaths of the Marys, though the elder Mary's brother-in-law Heinrich was killed by a falling tree, and several Buth children, some belonging to the elder Mary and her husband Johann, died young from disease, and possibly one in a house fire. The elder Mary lived well into her nineties, and there's no reason to believe she was murdered. The younger Mary has been described by those who could remember her as a kind but eccentric Seventh-Day Adventist, who never married. There's no word on if she had a loyal dog, though she did have lots of cats. The last living member of the Buth family, the younger Mary, left the farm in 1923 and moved to Milwaukee. She died in 1926. She was brought back to the farm and buried in the family cemetery alongside the rest of the Buths.

Given the fact the Buth farm is still private property and there's already such a problem with trespassing, I was hesitant even to include the farm in a legend tripper's guide like this. However, given its notoriety, it'd be conspicuous by its absence. Luckily, there are a couple of Buth Farm legends one can investigate without breaking the law. The stop sign near the farm entrance on Lovers Lane is supposed to indicate the whereabouts of the Marys. If the sign is blacked out, that means the ghosts are outside the house. If it appears normal, it means they're inside. The other legend involves the mailbox. When you drive past, sometimes it'll be on one side of the road, and other times, on the opposite. When driving past the Buth farm, please remember: trespassing ruins legend-tripping for everyone.

Bizarre Fact

The Mary Buth Farm haunting was featured in a 2006 independent horror film called *The Legend Trip*, by Milwaukee director Jason Satterfield. The film supposedly had a budget of only twenty thousand dollars.

The movie is a fun and gory yet somewhat hard-to-follow popcorn flick about a group of teens investigating the urban legends surrounding the farm, legends that involve gangsters, kidnappings, and insane doctors. Basically, it has nothing at all to do with the real legends of the Mary Buth Farm. That doesn't mean it can't be a guilty little pleasure for us real-life legend trippers, though.

Directions

From Milwaukee and Fond du Lac: Take HWY 41/45 to Germantown. Exit at HWY 167 E/Mequon Road, and head east.

From Madison: Take HWY 151 to Columbus. Exit at HWY 60, and follow it east. Take HWY 41 south to Germantown. Exit at HWY 167 E/Mequon Road, and head east.

Once in Germantown: From Mequon Road, turn north onto Country Aire Drive. Turn right onto CTY F/Freistadt Road. Turn left onto Mary Buth Lane. The house is the first driveway on the right after Lovers Lane.

Hubertus: Fox and Hounds Restaurant

The woman was ill, or so they thought. She stood leaning against the wall of the Fox and Hounds, mumbling to herself. Her skin was extremely pale, her breathing heavy and labored. The waitstaff quickly called management, and Dan Schneiter, a Fox and Hounds employee of twenty years, arrived on the scene. When he asked if she needed any assistance, she merely replied, "Such energy. I can feel it."

I stood in Fox and Hounds some years after the incident, as Schneiter recalled that night.

After regaining her composure, the woman identified herself as a psychic with a résumé that included various criminal cases for the Los Angeles Police Department. What was the source of this energy she felt? The psychic pointed to a photo of former owner Ray Wolf, which was hanging on the wall. The only problem was Ray Wolf had been dead for decades.

"After she pointed to the picture, she said, 'And he's standing behind the bar watching us right now,'" said Schneiter. The bar she pointed to was the building's original bar, the one behind which Ray Wolf died of natural causes. That's information Dan felt would be hard for her to come by. Dan didn't need a psychic detective from LA to confirm what he'd known for two decades, though. Ray Wolf was still very much a part of the Fox and Hounds.

The Fox and Hounds is one of the oldest buildings in Washington County. Originally built as a one-room log cabin in 1845, the building has had numerous additions and is now a charming patchwork behemoth. Ray Wolf bought the original log cabin in 1929 and turned it into a hunting lodge for himself and his fellow equestrians. When Ray wasn't hunting, he painted or traveled. Wolf regularly followed the various circuses that would winter in Wisconsin. Worried about leaving his wife, Alta, home with nothing to do, Ray converted the lodge into a restaurant, and that's what it's been ever since.

Image courtesy of Washington County Historical Society.

Ray Wolf, outdoorsman, artist, entrepreneur, and poltergeist. At least, that's a title given to him by Dan, and rightfully so if it is indeed Mr. Wolf who's responsible for the activity at the rural Hubertus eatery. Ray seems to love throwing objects around. "A few years ago, we used metal dish covers on all the food. Late one night, when no one was in the kitchen, we heard all this crashing. When we investigated, we found that the covers had been tossed all around the room," said Schneiter.

Schneiter then recalled one of Ray's more subtle manifestations. "We have wedding parties here a lot, and once, this one woman was very particular. Each guest had to have a name plate at their seat. We finally got all the name plates in all the right places. We left the dining room for a moment. When we came back, all the name plates were in little piles in the middle of the tables."

Back when Dan used to close the restaurant late at night, he'd frequently hear pacing from the empty upstairs apartment where Ray used to live. "When I'd finish up, I'd knock on the ceiling and say, 'It's all right; I'm leaving now, Ray!' and the pacing would stop."

I wondered to myself what Ray's motivation for the haunting was, but before I could ask, Schneiter answered my question.

"When the psychic was here, she said that Ray gets active when he's worried about the place. Back when there was a lot of activity, the former owners were letting the place [fall into disrepair]. Ever since the new owners renovated, it's been pretty quiet."

Ray Wolf must have loved the Fox and Hounds. He filled it with his collection of antiques and his paintings—a gallery was once part of the building. He lived there, he socialized there, and he died there. And now, he seemingly haunts there as well.

Ghosts like Ray Wolf make me hope that all this paranormal jazz is for real. I like to think that when I die, I could still linger in the place that matters to me most. Of course, I'm not certain if the owner of Sal's Pizza is accepting applications for a ghost.

Bizarre Fact

A couple of Ray's paintings still hang in the Fox and Hounds. One, a portrait of hunting dogs, is even said to contain hidden ghostly faces. When I visited, I looked at the painting and picked out several very easily. It's unclear if Ray intended this when he created the painting, or if it's merely coincidence.

Most of Ray's work was circus paintings. Many of these were donated to the Circus World Museum in Baraboo, Wisconsin, when he passed away. Ray's circus paintings are famous now, but while he was alive, he only sold one painting. Hollywood Director Cecil B. DeMille met Ray during the filming of *The Greatest Show on Earth* and purchased a painting titled *Belligerent Elephants*.

Directions

From Milwaukee and Fond du Lac: Take HWY 41 to Richfield. Exit at HWY 167 W/Holy Hill Road, and head west.

From Madison: Take HWY 151 to Columbus. Exit at HWY 60, and follow it east. Turn right onto HWY 83/S Main Street. Follow HWY 83. Turn left onto HWY 167/Holy Hill Road.

Once in Hubertus: From Holy Hill Road, turn south onto Friess Lake Road. The restaurant is on the left; watch for the signs.

Section III: Southern Washington County

Hubertus: Hogsback Road

The legend of the Goat Man is a rite of passage for the children of Washington County. For generations, this particularly gruesome legend has been told and retold around campfires.

Had I heard about it as a child, I likely would have had nightmares for weeks. Luckily, given my status as a transplant to the area, I was in my twenties when I first heard this disturbing tale via the Washington County Historical Society's Halloween program "Ghosts of Washington County." While the Goat Man has two drastically different origins (see "Goat Man Road" in section 1), this one is most often told. This is my retelling of the popular legend.

The Goat Man first began terrorizing the land shortly after the Civil War. A young soldier had recently returned home from the battlefield and was driving down Hogsback Road with his new bride. Even today, the road is treacherous and winding, as it is built on top of a narrow, glacial esker. Traveling up and down the hilly landscape proved too much for their shabby covered wagon, and one of the wheels splintered beneath them.

The young man was unable to repair the wheel himself. After kissing his young bride good-bye, he instructed her to remain safely under the canopy of the wagon. He'd see her soon, and he'd bring help, he promised.

The sun began to set over the isolated countryside. Night came. Hours passed with not a sign of the soldier's return.

It was so quiet and lonely in the broken little wagon. The young woman began to nod off in spite of herself. Just as sleep was about to take her, she awoke in a cold sweat. Something was moving in the thick darkness outside the wagon—something large.

Coarse bleating and heavy snuffling came from the woods. The sounds got louder. Closer. Panic raced down her spine. The snuffling was just outside the wagon. An overwhelming urge came upon her. She found herself easing toward the entrance. She didn't want to look, but she had to.

She slowly drew open the canopy with trembling hands. In the moonlight, she could make out a fearsome form. A huge, hairy creature with the body of a man and the head of a goat stood just in front of her.

She screamed and scrambled to the back of the wagon. Expecting the beast to enter at any moment, she did the only thing she could do. She prayed. The beast never came for her.

After what seemed an eternity, light returned. Cautiously stepping outside, the young woman spied large prints made by cloven hooves around the outside of the wagon. Her courage returning with the light of day, she followed them. The tracks stopped beneath a tree just behind the wagon and then turned toward the woods. The exposed roots of the tree were covered in a thick, red liquid. She looked up. There was her husband draped across a limb of the tree, his throat ripped open.

Apparently, the Goat Man learned a valuable lesson that night: broken-down travelers make for an easy kill. Since that fateful night, the Goat Man has caused travelers to crash over the high esker that is Hogsback Road. Moving so quickly as to appear a blur, he makes cars careen off the road as drivers try to avoid whatever just darted out in front of them. The vehicles are always empty, the bodies of the motorists never found.

Now, imagine hearing that yarn in the woods at night when you're six years old. Linda Godfrey's book *Strange Wisconsin: More Badger State Weirdness* reports that as of 2007, the community was making efforts to clean up the bloody legend. Newer versions of the story paint Goat Man as an ecologically concerned, friendly woodland creature. While this isn't nearly as thrilling as the original tale, it is truer to the motivations of the mythological satyrs, which is what many have labeled the Goat Man. This politically correct, green version of the legend hasn't stuck. Kids still love to scare each other with the original, bloody legend of the Goat Man.

Section III: Southern Washington County

The Ghosts of Hogsback

Goat Man or no, Hogsback Road is treacherous. One particular area alongside the road is littered with the rusting ruins of vehicles that were traveling too fast for the curve and plunged off the esker.

The spirits of these reckless motorists are said to haunt the deep places where they lost their lives. Apparitions can be seen and inexplicable sounds and smells experienced. If you do go out to Hogsback Road in search of the unexplained, do be cautious. You wouldn't want to join these poor lost souls, would you?

The Hanging Tree

There was once an enormous oak tree on Hogsback Road that kids referred to as "the Hanging Tree." This was supposedly the tree where the young bride found her husband's bloody remains.

According to people who grew up near Hogsback Road in the 1970s, each Halloween, teens would hang a dummy from it in effigy to celebrate the legend of the Goat Man. Rebellious youth also decorated the tree with spray-painted pentagrams. I've been told that at some point, the tree was cut down because of the negative attention it attracted. In a way, that poor tree became just another victim of the Goat Man.

The Hook-Man Cuts In!

The Goat Man isn't the only murderous fiend associated with Hogsback. There is also the Hook-Man. Just about everyone has heard a story about a psychopath stalking lustful teenagers with a murderous implement for an appendage. Hook stories have been around for decades, all across America.

While the variations of this tale are legion, the basic details rarely change. A young couple parks in some secluded, wooded area, and things get steamy, until a strange noise is heard outside the car. The girl becomes fearful—and a lot less keen on shedding her clothes—so the boy goes outside to investigate. The story usually ends with the boy hanging from his neck above the car with his throat slit, leaving the girl to drive panic-stricken into night, usually with the murderer's bloody hook-hand stuck in the car's door.

According to people who grew up near Hubertus in the 1970s and 1980s, the Hook-Man lurked around Hogsback Road. It was said he lived in an ancient, rundown house with an old tin roof. If you parked on Hogsback to make-out, the Hook-Man would find you, cut your throat with his hook, and leave you hanging from the trees.

I drove down Hogsback with several adults who remember the stories, even the house where he was said to dwell. We were unable to locate the house. Either it has been torn down or is no longer recognizable.

The similarities between the Goat Man and the Hook-Man legends are obvious. Both savagely rip out the throats of their victims and leave them in trees. The only real difference is the former enjoys killing travelers, the latter, lovers. No reason to worry though, the Hook-Man is just fantasy, right? Well, not entirely.

In 1946 a man wearing a white mask began a killing spree in Texarkana, Texas. Several teenage couples were shot to death, and the girls were sexually assaulted and tortured before they were killed. The killer was nicknamed "the Phantom" by the press. While he didn't have a hook for a hand, these killings, commonly known as the "moonlight murders," are considered by many urban legend enthusiasts to be the origin of such "Lover's Lane" urban legends as the Hook-Man—which are thought to have started circulating in the 1950s.

While it's unlikely the Phantom killer of Texarkana could still be alive, much less stalking isolated areas of southeastern Wisconsin, I should point out he was never brought to justice. I suppose the moral of the story is *get a room*—unless it's at the Bates Motel, of course.

Directions

From Milwaukee and Fond du Lac: Take HWY 41 to Richfield. Exit at HWY 167 W/Holy Hill Road, and head west.

From Madison: Take HWY 151 to Columbus. Exit at HWY 60, and follow it east. Turn right onto HWY 83/S Main Street. Follow HWY 83. Turn left onto HWY 167/Holy Hill Road.

Once in Hubertus: From Holy Hill Road, turn south onto St. Augustine Road. At the stop sign, go left onto Hogsback Road (right is St. Augustine Road). Hogsback Road ends at Friess Lake Road/Hubertus Road.

Selected Bibliography

Anderson, Jack H. *Dark Lanterns: An American Lynching*. West Bend, WI: Dark Lanterns Press, 1987.

Armstrong, William Ayres. *Miracle Hill: A Legendary Tale of Wisconsin*. Milwaukee, WI: Cramer, Aikens, and Cramer Engravers and Printers, 1889.

Benson, Dan. "School Buries Cemetery Collection." *Milwaukee Journal Sentinel*, October 26, 2003.

"B. Goetter Gone to Rest." *West Bend Democrat*, September 25, 1889.

Birmingham, Robert A., and Leslie E. Eisenberg. *Indian Mounds of Wisconsin*. Madison, WI: University of Wisconsin Press, 2000.

Boatman, John. *Wisconsin American Indian History and Culture: A Survey of Selected Aspect*. Milwaukee, WI: University of Wisconsin-Milwaukee, 1993.

Chandler, Kurt. "Where the Wild Things Are." *Milwaukee Magazine* 36 (2011): 70–76.

Derrick, Linda, and Annette Krebs. "Growing Up down the Road from the Mill." *Richfield Historical Society Newsletter* 14.

Drissel, Richard H. *A History of the Village of Barton, Washington County, Wisconsin*. West Bend, WI: Richard H. Drissel, 1997.

Foley, Ellen. "Lizard Mound Skull Turns Up in Waupaca." *West Bend Daily News*, August 7, 1975.

Freckmann, Kermit. "Hagner Indian Mounds." *The Wisconsin Archeologist* 23 (1942): 1–16.

Geringer, Joseph. Trutv.com. *The Phantom Killer: Texarkana Moonlight Murders*. Accessed August 06, 2012. http://www.trutv.com/library/crime/serial_killers/unsolved/texarkana/index_1.html

Germantown Historical Society (Germantown, WI). "Walking Tour—Dheinsville Settlement Park." Accessed June 17, 2012. http://www.bastbellmuseum.com/walking_tour.html.

Ghosts of America. "West Bend, Wisconsin Ghost Sightings." Accessed June 17, 2012. http://www.ghostsofamerica.com/5/Wisconsin_West_Bend_ghost_sightings.html.

Ghostvillage. "Haunted High School." Accessed June 17, 2012. http://www.ghostvillage.com/encounters/2004/06302004.shtml.

Godfrey, Linda S. Strange. *Wisconsin: More Badger State Weirdness*. Madison, WI: Trail Books, 2007.

Goldstein, Lynne. *The Southeastern Wisconsin Archaeological Project: 1982–1983*. Milwaukee, WI: University of Wisconsin-Milwaukee Archaeological Research Laboratory, 1983.

Jackson Historical Society. *The History of Jackson, Wisconsin, 1843–1976*. Germantown, WI: Germantown Press, 1976.

Krueger, Mary, and Lee Krueger. *The Town of West Bend*. West Bend, WI: Mary and Lee Krueger, 2008.

Lee, Patrick, and Anne Spitza. "Only Ghosts Stumble off of Saloon's Bar Stools." *Milwaukee Journal*, October 26, 1984.

Morgano, Anthony. "The Town Ghost." *The Corkboard*, December 6, 2010.

Nichols, Mike. "Purported Ghosts Frightfully Ordinary." *Milwaukee Journal Sentinel*, October 5, 2000.

Norman, Michael, and Beth Scott. *Haunted Wisconsin*. Minocqua, WI: Heartland Press, 1980.

Parsons, Lee A. "Unique Display of Skeleton at Lizard State Park." *Wisconsin Archeologist* 41 (1960): 56–65.

Peterson, Mark. "Celebrating Regner and Public Parks; 'Thriller' Event Re-Creates Recreation." *West Bend Daily News*, July 31, 2010.

Quickert, Carl. *Washington County, Wisconsin Past and Present*. Chicago, IL: S. J. Clark Publishing Company, 1912.

Selected Bibliography

"Restat Building: A Ghost in the Works." *West Bend Daily News*, February 15, 2006.

Seibel, Jaqcueline. "Tower Hosted Hose Hoisting." *West Bend Daily News*, December 16, 1996.

Shadowlands (The). "Haunted Places in Wisconsin." Accessed June 17, 2012. http://www.theshadowlands.net/places/ wisconsin.htm.

Shekleton, Margaret. *Bending in Season: History of the North American Province of the Sisters of the Divine Savior, 1895 to 1985*. Madison, WI: University of Wisconsin Press, 1985.

Slinger Centennial Committee. *Slinger Historical Album: Schleisingerville to Slinger 125 Years*. Slinger, WI: Slinger Advancement Association, 1969.

Washington County Historical Society, Wisconsin. "St. Agnes Historic Convent and School." Accessed June 17, 2012. http://www.historyisfun.com/wordpress/?page_id=518.

West Bend Bicentennial Committee. *West Bend Historical Album*. West Bend, WI: Serigraph Sales and Manufacturing Company, 1976.

Williams, Dorothy E. *The Spirit of West Bend*. Madison, WI: Straus Printing Company, 1980.

Wisconsinosity. "Washington County." Accessed June 17, 2012. http://www.wisconsinosity.com/Washington/washington.htm.

About the Author

Photo by Charlie Hintz of Mental Shed Studios.

J. Nathan Couch grew up in the foothills of Northeast Georgia's Appalachian Mountains. Given the area's rich tradition of ghost stories and folklore, it's no wonder he developed a passion for the bizarre and the unexplained.

Nathan is currently a resident of West Bend, Wisconsin. He is a published writer and poet and a member of the Wisconsin Writers' Association, the Washington County Writers' Club, and the Moraine Writers' Guild. Presently, he's a regular contributor at WisconsinSickness.com, where he interviews authors, burlesque dancers, circus freaks, and other folks who are genuinely worth reading about.

Ordering and Contact Information

To order more copies of this books, contact Nathan, learn about taking guided Washington County ghost walks, or arrange investigations with the Paranormal Investigation and Research Society (PIRS), please visit www.JNathanCouch.com.

Made in the
USA
Columbia, SC